FIFTH GRADE SURVIVAL GUIDE

Fun Tips, Exam Strategies, & Puzzles To Conquer 5th Grade Like a Superhero!

Bobbie Anderson Jr

Copyright 2025 by Bobbie Anderson Jr.
- ALL Rights Reserved

In no way is it legal to reproduce, duplicate, or transmit any part of this document in either electronic means or in printed format. Recording of this publication is strictly prohibited and any storage of this document is not allowed unless with written permission from the publisher.

Thank you for buying our book and supporting our mission to provide accessible resources for everyone!

Instructions for Word Search Puzzles

- Hidden words are key vocabulary of each chapter
- Some words are combined. For example, "fifth grade" is hidden as "fifhgrade".
- Words are hidden in forward, horizontal, vertical, in reverse, and four diagonal directions (top-left, top-right, bottom-left, bottom-right).
- STUCK? The parenthesis shows combined words.

To avoid any potential bleed-through while solving word search puzzles with certain pens or markers, simply place a blank sheet of thicker paper behind the page you're working on.

Whether your child is excited, nervous, or somewhere in between, this guide offers fun ways to help your fifth grader succeed in school while preparing them for the next stage of their educational journey.

Each chapter ends with a fun word search puzzle that reinforces key concepts, making learning enjoyable and helping kids retain knowledge effectively.

LET'S GO!

Table of Contents

Chapter 1: How to Crush the First Day of Fifth Grade 7

Chapter 2: How to Pick the Right Friends in Fifth Grade 15

Chapter 3: How to Handle Disagreements in the Fifth Grade Classroom 23

Chapter 4: How to Handle Disagreements on the Playground in Fifth Grade 31

Chapter 5: How to Ask the Right Questions in Fifth Grade 39

Chapter 6: How to Rock Small Group Work in Fifth Grade 47

Chapter 7: How to Succeed in Studying History in Fifth Grade 55

Chapter 8: How to Master Fifth Grade Math 63

Chapter 9: How to Succeed in Reading in Fifth Grade 71

Chapter 10: How to Succeed in Fifth Grade P.E. 79

Chapter 11: How to Succeed in Science in Fifth Grade 87

Chapter 12: How to Succeed in Writing in Fifth Grade 95

Chapter 13: How to Master Homework in Fifth Grade 103

Chapter 14: How to Study for Exams in Fifth Grade 111

Word Search Solutions .... 119 - 133

BELONGS TO

....

Chapter 1

How to Crush the First Day of Fifth Grade

Hey, future fifth grader! The first day of fifth grade is a big deal—you're not just starting another school year; you're stepping into the final year of elementary school! This is your time to shine, take on new responsibilities, and set the stage for an incredible year. Feeling nervous? Excited? Both? Don't worry—you've got this. Let's talk about how to handle the first day of fifth grade with confidence and make it a day to remember.

1. Know That You're the Big Kid Now
Fifth grade means you're one of the oldest and most experienced students in the school. Younger kids might look up to you, and teachers expect you to be a role model. Don't stress—this is your chance to show everyone how awesome you are.

Real-Life Scenario:
A second grader in the hallway drops their art project. Instead of walking past, you stop and help them pick it up. They look up at you like you're a hero. You're already rocking your fifth-grade status!

2. Get Organized Before School Starts
Preparation is key to feeling confident on the first day. Pack your backpack the night before with all your supplies, like notebooks, pencils, and any forms your parents filled out. Being ready means you won't have to scramble in the morning.

Real-Life Scenario:
Last year, you forgot to bring your scissors on the first day of art class and had to borrow a pair. This year, you double-check your supply list the night before. When the teacher says, "Take out your scissors," you're ready!

3. Show Up with a Positive Attitude

The way you start your day can set the tone for the rest of the year. Walk into the classroom with a smile, say hello to your teacher, and greet your classmates. A positive vibe is contagious.

Real-Life Scenario:

You walk into class and see a classmate looking nervous in the corner. You smile and say, "Hey, are you excited for this year?" They nod and start to relax. Later, they thank you for making them feel welcome.

4. Pay Attention to the Rules and Routines

Fifth grade often comes with new rules, routines, and responsibilities. Listen closely when your teacher explains how things will work, like the schedule, classroom jobs, and how homework is handled.

Real-Life Scenario:

Your teacher explains that turning in homework late means losing points. You make a mental note to double-check your planner every night. By staying on top of your assignments, you avoid the dreaded "missing homework" list.

5. Find Your Go-To Spot

Whether it's your desk, a cubby, or a locker, make your space your own. Keep it neat and organized so you can find what you need without stress.

Real-Life Scenario:

You notice that your neighbor's desk is already a mess of crumpled papers. Meanwhile, you've neatly arranged your notebooks and pencils. When it's time to grab your math book, you find it in seconds, while your neighbor is still searching.

6. Be Open to Meeting New People

Even if you already have friends, the first day is a great time to connect with new classmates. Sit with someone you don't know at lunch or during an activity—you might just meet your new best friend.

Real-Life Scenario:
You sit next to a new student during a classroom icebreaker. They mention they love skateboarding, and you say, "Me too! Do you know any cool tricks?" By the end of the activity, you've already made plans to compare moves at recess.

7. Don't Stress About the Schedule

The first day can feel like a whirlwind of new classes, teachers, and subjects. If you're unsure where to go or what to do, don't panic—teachers know it's all new, and they're there to help.

Real-Life Scenario:
You forget which classroom to go to for science. Instead of stressing, you ask a classmate, and they point you in the right direction. You make it on time and realize it wasn't such a big deal after all.

8. Take on a Leadership Role

Fifth grade often comes with more responsibility, like helping with classroom jobs, leading group projects, or mentoring younger students. Step up and show your teacher you're ready for the challenge.

Real-Life Scenario:
Your teacher asks for a volunteer to explain how the new recycling system works. You raise your hand and confidently share the steps with the class. Your teacher smiles and says, "Great job!" You feel proud of stepping up.

9. Be Flexible and Go with the Flow
The first day doesn't always go perfectly. Maybe there's a last-minute schedule change or a class activity that doesn't go as planned. Stay positive and adapt—it's all part of the adventure.

Real-Life Scenario:
Your class is supposed to have gym outside, but it starts raining. Instead of complaining, you join your classmates in an indoor game of four corners. By the end, everyone is laughing and having a blast.

10. Write Down Something Good About the Day
At the end of the first day, take a moment to think about what went well. Maybe you made a new friend, discovered your teacher has a great sense of humor, or loved the cool math activity.

Real-Life Scenario:
You write in your notebook, "I got picked to share my favorite summer memory, and everyone laughed at my funny camping story." Reflecting on the positives helps you feel excited for the rest of the year.

11. Be Yourself

You don't need to pretend to be someone you're not. The best way to make friends and connect with your teacher is by being your true self.

Real-Life Scenario:
You love drawing but worry about what others might think. When the teacher asks for volunteers to create a poster for the class rules, you raise your hand and offer to illustrate it. Your classmates compliment your art, and you feel proud of being you.

Final Thought
The first day of fifth grade is your chance to start fresh, meet new people, and show everyone what makes you unique. By staying positive, being prepared, and embracing the challenges, you'll set yourself up for an amazing year. Remember, fifth grade is your time to shine—so go out there, give it your all, and make it a day to remember. You've got this!

Chapter 1 How to Crush the First Day of Fifth Grade

```
E K B I N E M P Z A Q P Q V K V E I Z N W Q S
Y J F N Q Z L R G O N J W O M V L E K W A D K
L C N K G F S D D X W E P U I G U E B G I G Z
U I N D Q A F X X A S Z H T M R L Q M Z L B E
K D L E F B O I X Q Y V I D N I U D Y S E Z G
L C E W L J E V E F X S Y O U R S E L F T F R
O V A U M O X C E F O Z I M L Y O U T O F B J
S B D K N H R O Z P G T U W K D S Z V P F W W
B V E B U B I C M H A K Z O V X E A V I A O V
J V R T B W E X K R J A M V M U O S F T W F U
C D S O G A L P A F L E X I B L E T T E F H A
J C H V H S C P A E Q F V I S C H I P I W M V
P V I Y V E E B K Z A V X P Y G T Y R X N D S
Z I P E B R P N Q L Q H G J R U K S I O S J J
O V G G P L L G I F B J I A D M T P B E V U X
Y T T Y Q H F Q Y T G F D E H D U S G W W P V
O K C D H L A E Y U U E Y H A Y P N B M R Z T
V A E C Q B N R M S Z O N Y S W E C W U K T R
N L N F X I R C G C R J R G T L N M O H T K Y
K T N U H M V G E S P V E K L L N H T O S Y T
G W O S H I Z F Y U U O G A Y Q E F O J V O Y
R Y C E K O T I M A F L H T K S C H E D U L E
V E O Q W I S K W D B C F T X L C X O B L T G
```

attitude	flexible	role
challenges	leadership	routines
connect	oldest	schedule
fifthgrade (fifth grade)	Positive	shine
firstday (first day)	Preparation	yourself

Chapter 2

How to Pick the Right Friends in Fifth Grade

Hey, fifth-grade friendship expert! By now, you've probably had a lot of practice making friends, but fifth grade is a whole new level. You're older, wiser, and ready to build friendships that really matter. This year, you'll meet new people, hang out with old friends, and maybe deal with some tricky situations. So how do you find friends who are fun to be with, kind, and help you be the best version of yourself? This chapter is packed with real-life fifth-grade scenarios and ideas to help you choose the right friends. Let's get started!

1. Find Friends Who Match Your Energy

Best friends are people who share your vibe. If you're super energetic, find someone who loves to join in your games. If you prefer quiet activities, look for someone who enjoys reading or drawing during recess.

Real-Life Scenario:

You're always moving and love playing tag at recess. You notice another kid running as fast as you are, dodging everyone with a huge grin. You team up, and suddenly, you've got a new partner in crime for every recess.

2. Look for Loyalty

In fifth grade, loyalty matters more than ever. A good friend sticks with you, even when things get tough. If someone talks behind your back or leaves you out on purpose, they might not be the right friend.

Real-Life Scenario:

During a class debate, someone teases you about your answer. Your friend says, "Hey, that's not cool," and backs you up. You realize they're the kind of friend you can count on.

3. Watch How They Handle Problems
Conflict happens in every friendship, but the way someone handles it says a lot about them. Look for friends who are willing to apologize, compromise, and work things out.

Real-Life Scenario:
You and a friend both want to be the team captain in kickball. They say, "Let's take turns being captain each game." You realize they're mature and know how to keep things fair.

4. Choose Friends Who Make You Laugh
Fifth grade can get busy and stressful, so friends who make you laugh are the best. Humor can turn a tough day into a good one.

Real-Life Scenario:
You're stuck inside on a rainy day, and everyone's grumpy. Your friend starts doing silly impressions of your teacher (in a respectful way), and soon the whole group is laughing. That's the kind of friend you want around!

5. Find Friends Who Challenge You—in a Good Way
The right friends push you to try new things and be your best self. They encourage you to study harder, try a new hobby, or go for that part in the class play.

Real-Life Scenario:
You're nervous about entering the school spelling bee, but your friend says, "You're amazing at spelling! You should totally go for it." Their encouragement gives you the confidence to sign up—and you make it to the final round!

6. Notice How You Feel Around Them

A good friend makes you feel happy, supported, and relaxed. If you feel stressed, ignored, or like you're not good enough around someone, it might be time to rethink that friendship.

Real-Life Scenario:
You hang out with one group that always jokes about your shoes, and it makes you feel bad. Later, you spend time with a friend who compliments your drawing skills and makes you laugh. It's clear who makes you feel better about yourself.

7. Be Friends with People Who Respect Differences

Not all your friends need to be just like you. Some of the best friendships come from learning about and appreciating each other's differences.

Real-Life Scenario:
You love sports, but your new friend is all about building robots. Instead of ignoring each other's interests, you show them your basketball moves, and they teach you how to code a robot. You both learn something new—and have a blast.

8. Avoid Drama Magnets

Some people thrive on drama—spreading rumors, stirring up arguments, or always creating chaos. Friends like that can make your year stressful, so it's okay to step away from them.

Real-Life Scenario:
You notice one classmate always talks about who's "not cool" and tries to get you to pick sides in arguments. Instead, you choose to hang out with someone who stays out of the drama and focuses on fun.

9. Build a Friendship That Grows

Fifth grade is all about growing as a person, and the right friends grow with you. They'll cheer you on when you try new things and adjust when your interests change.

Real-Life Scenario:
Last year, you and a friend were obsessed with Pokémon, but now you're getting into skateboarding. They say, "I've never tried skateboarding—teach me!" They're excited to grow with you instead of clinging to the past.

10. Be a Friend Magnet

The best way to find great friends is to be a great friend. Show kindness, listen, and treat people the way you want to be treated.

Real-Life Scenario:
During a group project, you notice one person hasn't said much. You ask, "What do you think we should do?" They smile and share an idea. Later, they tell you, "Thanks for including me." Your thoughtfulness makes you a friend magnet.

11. Trust Your Gut

Sometimes, you just get a feeling about someone—good or bad. If you feel like someone is kind and trustworthy, go for it. If something feels off, it's okay to keep your distance.

Real-Life Scenario:
A new student invites you to join their table at lunch, and you instantly feel welcome. You trust your gut, and by the end of the week, they're one of your closest friends.

12. Celebrate Your Friendships

Once you find great friends, appreciate them! Say thank you, share your favorite activities, and be there for them when they need you.

Real-Life Scenario:
Your friend helps you study for a tough math test, so you make them a homemade thank-you card. They smile and say, "This made my day!" Small acts of appreciation strengthen your bond.

Final Thought
Fifth grade is your chance to build friendships that matter. The right friends will make you laugh, cheer you on, and stand by you no matter what. Remember, lasting friendships take time, kindness, and effort—but they're worth it. So go out there, meet new people, and surround yourself with friends who bring out the best in you. You've got this, fifth grader!

Chapter 2 How to Pick the Right Friends in Fifth Grade

```
K V U L T U E N B H J J J F I N S J J G M H I
T A L O W C B X U H V S N U Q C F H Q J C Y B
H A N Y C J I E C Z N H W G F L A O G O E S P
V C K A U H V E O D V P A F W A V U Z Y B K V
B I M L V G J X M A T O C X W K X O E G S U K
U C A T J R J C P P R I D U X P Z O N F W C X
R Z K Y F E P O R I U C U I G X Y H D A O I W
O R L A M W L I O H S D K M R Q G E I D R P A
H C R D I O M N M S T B A M A R D X F W G C C
G R X V G I T C I D S F T R H G W Y H K Y Q C
E D S I K J S O S N T D O P H T I A Y Z X D X
Z S Z W G H E Y E E I M T U M F I L S A U B A
I E B X Y Y C F F I W I L U S P Q M M L Z S I
P K S L W O N Z A R G X R B I O H E H K C E A
J N D U N T E P V F I P F R Q N G Y Z C Z Q B
S Y N J D V R V R Y T H C K O A O W V I I B Y
K U E F P W E M C T J U O E R P P F W P N N S
E P I V C J F N W Y D J Y U P I T V V G L T F
F Y R X D L F E S U P P O R T E D J L P T B F
D J F U O F I U L Q N C D M N H L A U G H U U
F Q I X L F D V T S N K A J B J G K L A C A V
X K F Z S U N Y J E R Y X C M M H I O O R Z Q
A F I V P L U Y M A D N Y A V L K P R J C U S
```

apologize	friends	pick
compromise	friendship	right
differences	grows	supported
drama	laugh	trust
encourage	loyalty	vibe

Chapter 3

How to Handle Disagreements in the Fifth-Grade Classroom

Hey, fifth-grade peacemaker! Disagreements happen—it's just part of working and learning with other people. But by fifth grade, you're ready to handle conflicts like a pro. Whether it's about group projects, class rules, or just someone borrowing your favorite marker without asking, this chapter is packed with ideas to help you manage disagreements in a calm, fair, and awesome way. Let's get started!

1. Stay Calm (Even When You're Frustrated)
The first step to handling any disagreement is to stay cool. If you're upset, take a deep breath or count to five before saying anything. This gives you time to think before you react.

Real-Life Scenario:
You're in a group project, and one teammate keeps interrupting you. Instead of snapping, you take a deep breath and say, "Can I finish my idea? Then we can talk about yours." Staying calm keeps the discussion on track.

2. Use "I" Statements
When you're upset, it's easy to start blaming others. Instead, talk about how you feel by using "I" statements, like "I feel" or "I think." It's less likely to make the other person defensive.

Real-Life Scenario:
Your classmate grabs your eraser without asking. Instead of saying, "You always take my stuff!" you say, "I feel frustrated when you take my things without asking. Can you ask next time?" Now they know how you feel, and they're more likely to listen.

3. Listen to the Other Person's Side
Disagreements aren't just about your perspective, there's always another side to the story. Let the other person explain their point of view before jumping to conclusions.

Real-Life Scenario:
You think a classmate cut in line for lunch. Instead of accusing them, you ask, "Why did you step in front of me?" They explain they thought you were saving their spot. Now you understand it was a misunderstanding, not rudeness.

4. Find a Win-Win Solution
The best way to solve a disagreement is to find a solution that works for everyone. This might mean compromising or coming up with a creative new idea.

Real-Life Scenario:
You and a friend both want to be the leader of a classroom activity. Instead of arguing, you suggest, "How about we take turns leading different parts?" Now you're both happy, and the activity runs smoothly.

5. Don't Bring Others Into It (Unless You Need To)
It's tempting to get other classmates involved in your disagreement, but this can make things worse. Solve the problem one-on-one unless it's something serious that needs a teacher's help.

Real-Life Scenario:
You and a partner disagree about how to decorate your project. Instead of asking your friends to pick sides, you talk it through together and come up with a plan you both like.

6. Use Humor to Lighten the Mood
Sometimes, a little humor can make a tense situation feel less serious. Just make sure your joke is kind and not aimed at the other person.

Real-Life Scenario:
You and a classmate argue about who gets the last blue crayon. You hold it up and say, "Maybe we should flip a coin—or arm-wrestle for it!" Everyone laughs, and you end up sharing the crayon.

7. Respect the Classroom Rules
Your teacher probably has rules about how to solve problems in the classroom. Follow those rules so everyone stays respectful and focused on learning.

Real-Life Scenario:
Your teacher says, "If you can't agree, raise your hand, and I'll help." When you and a group member can't agree on how to split the work, you ask the teacher for advice. They help you divide the tasks evenly, and the project moves forward.

8. Take a Break if Things Get Heated
If a disagreement gets too intense, it's okay to take a break. Step away for a minute to cool down and think about what you really want to say.

Real-Life Scenario:
You're arguing with a classmate about whose turn it is to present. Instead of continuing to argue, you say, "Let's take a break and talk about it in a few minutes." After the break, you both feel calmer and work it out easily.

9. Be Willing to Apologize

If you realize you've made a mistake or hurt someone's feelings, a sincere apology can fix things quickly. Saying "I'm sorry" shows you care about the other person's feelings.

Real-Life Scenario:

You snap at a friend during group work because you're stressed. Later, you say, "I'm sorry for snapping. I was feeling overwhelmed." Your friend forgives you, and you both move on.

10. Learn When to Let It Go

Not every disagreement needs a long conversation. Sometimes, it's better to let small things go and focus on what really matters.

Real-Life Scenario:

A classmate makes a joke about your handwriting. It annoys you, but you realize they weren't trying to be mean. Instead of starting an argument, you shrug it off and focus on finishing your work.

11. Ask for Help When You Need It

If the problem is too big to solve on your own or someone is being unkind, it's okay to ask your teacher or another adult for help.

Real-Life Scenario:

A group member keeps ignoring your ideas and refuses to let you participate. You talk to your teacher, who helps set clear rules for teamwork. Now everyone gets a fair chance to contribute.

12. Learn From Every Disagreement

Every time you solve a disagreement, you're building important skills. Think about what worked and what didn't, so you're even better at handling conflicts next time.

Real-Life Scenario:
You and a friend argue about which game to play at recess. You suggest taking turns choosing games, and it works! You realize compromise is a great way to solve disagreements.

Final Thought
Disagreements are a normal part of fifth grade, but how you handle them can make a big difference. By staying calm, listening to others, and finding fair solutions, you'll build stronger friendships and make your classroom a happier place. Remember, being a peacemaker doesn't mean avoiding disagreements, it means solving them in a way that works for everyone. You've got this, fifth grader!

Chapter 3 How to Handle Disagreements in the Fifth Grade Classroom

```
A C R J S O Y L H L T Z N V Z G U M Y S U J G
Z D D N Y O N G R J I K O G P K B I V K U C D
K Q K M O Z T E O L N S B E G L E H W L O N I
A G V H N N M U O Y Q I T Z X V K U Q Z G M Z
E D X C R J B K S N U Q U E N A Z P F N D A Z
R S X F A E C O P J O D S M N J C R G H R G I
B J H F E E B G H P R N B O N N L F B T E G D
I C Q T L R S T N E M E E R G A S I D S S Q D
U F W Y Z I J Q A Z D P O G X V O R Q D P V W
Q M F E G Z P R U N N J S D I X Z K Q R E X G
M R E M F Q N W G N Z K Y B Z Y S B M L C R N
E W J K K X A E X A L W N H E T M O B V T F W
K T Q T J T Z I X R I A F V B M W J S G D T H
A P W M O F D C J M Q E Y M S O L U T I O N I
T E N F N R N C C R J N W X H U H S N G W O R
S F G V Q G O R E E H Y A U X H T R E U M W A
I Y I C E G C M Q S K R I M H K S R M U D E W
M F Q T T P E R S P E C T I V E V X E M C F F
C X A I U I H H F W H I X B Y M Y Y T Z Q T P
T A T Z D V N M N W E H D Q Z R Z Y A C A L M
G E K J R N B M I F N D B B K N U Y T J E Z Q
L M P H U M O R C S K E U X Y J D S S H T Q Y
W G V R S G U K R Q H W U Z Z O J E I M V A L
```

break	humor	mistake
calm	istatements (I statements)	oneonone (one on one)
disagreements	learn	perspective
fair	letitgo (let it go)	respect
help	listen	solution

Chapter 4

Handling Disagreements on the Playground in Fifth Grade

Hey there, playground peacemaker! The playground is one of the best places to let loose, have fun, and hang out with your friends. But let's face it—sometimes disagreements pop up. Maybe it's about who's playing by the rules, whose turn it is, or what game to play. The good news is fifth grade is the perfect time to learn how to handle playground conflicts like a pro. This chapter is packed with tips, real-life scenarios, and strategies to help you solve problems and get back to what really matters: having fun!

1. Stay Cool When Things Heat Up
It's easy to get upset during a disagreement, especially when you feel like you're being treated unfairly. But keeping your cool is the first step to solving any conflict. Take a deep breath, count to five, and remind yourself that it's not the end of the world.

Real-Life Scenario:
You're playing soccer, and someone calls a goal that you're sure didn't go in. Instead of shouting, "That's not fair!" you take a deep breath and say, "Let's talk about it. Can we check with someone else who saw the play?" Staying calm keeps things from escalating.

2. Use "We" Instead of "You"
When you're trying to solve a disagreement, saying "you did this" or "you're wrong" can make things worse. Instead, use words like "we" or "let's" to show you want to work together to fix the problem.

Real-Life Scenario:
You and your friends are arguing over who gets to be "it" in freeze tag. Instead of saying, "You always get to go first," you suggest, "Let's figure out a fair way to decide—maybe we can take turns or play rock-paper-scissors." Suddenly, the problem feels easier to solve.

3. Know When to Walk Away
Not every disagreement needs to be solved right away. If things are getting too heated, it's okay to take a break. Walking away gives everyone time to cool off and think about how to fix the problem.

Real-Life Scenario:
You and a friend are arguing about who won a race. They start shouting, and you can feel yourself getting mad too. You say, "Let's talk about this later—I don't want us to fight." After recess, you both apologize and move on.

4. Compromise Like a Pro
A compromise means finding a solution that works for everyone, even if it's not exactly what you wanted. In fifth grade, this skill is a game-changer for handling playground disagreements.

Real-Life Scenario:
Your group can't agree on whether to play kickball or capture the flag. You suggest, "What if we play kickball for the first half of recess and capture the flag for the second half?" Everyone agrees, and now you all get to enjoy both games.

5. Include Everyone

Sometimes, disagreements happen because someone feels left out. If you notice someone on the sidelines, try to include them. It can prevent problems before they start.

Real-Life Scenario:
You're organizing a basketball game, and someone complains that the teams aren't fair. You realize a few people haven't been picked yet, so you say, "Let's shuffle the teams and make sure everyone gets to play." The game goes smoothly, and no one feels left out.

6. Get Creative with Solutions

Sometimes, the best way to solve a disagreement is to think outside the box. Be creative and look for solutions that make the situation more fun instead of more frustrating.

Real-Life Scenario:
You're arguing with a friend about whether the ball was in or out during a volleyball game. Instead of continuing to argue, you say, "Let's just replay the point. That way, no one has to feel left out." Everyone agrees, and the game continues.

7. Apologize When You're Wrong

Owning up to your mistakes is a sign of maturity—and it can stop an argument in its tracks. If you realize you're wrong, don't be afraid to say sorry.

Real-Life Scenario:
You accuse someone of cheating during a four-square game, but later realize they were playing by the rules. You say, "I'm sorry for accusing you—I didn't understand the rule." They accept your apology, and you both go back to playing.

8. Ask for a Neutral Opinion
If you can't agree, find someone else to weigh in. A classmate or teacher can often help settle the disagreement.

Real-Life Scenario:
Your team can't decide if a player was tagged or not in a game of capture the flag. You ask a classmate who was watching the game, "Did you see what happened?" They explain what they saw, and everyone agrees to follow their call.

9. Be a Role Model
As a fifth-grader, younger kids might look up to you on the playground. Show them how to handle disagreements with kindness and fairness.

Real-Life Scenario:
You notice a group of younger kids arguing over who gets to use the swings. You step in and say, "Why don't you take turns? Each person can swing for five minutes." They follow your suggestion and thank you for helping.

10. Learn When to Let It Go
Not every disagreement needs to be solved. Sometimes, it's better to let small things go and focus on enjoying the rest of your day.

Real-Life Scenario:
You're playing tetherball, and your opponent claims they won the game. You know it was close, but instead of arguing, you say, "Good game!" and move on to another activity. You feel proud of keeping the peace.

Final Thought
Disagreements on the playground don't have to ruin your recess. By staying calm, working together, and being open to creative solutions, you can handle conflicts like a true fifth-grade leader. Remember, the goal isn't to "win" the argument—it's to make sure everyone has fun and feels included. So, the next time a disagreement pops up, use these tips to solve the problem and get back to what really matters: playing, laughing, and enjoying your time outside. You've got this, peacemaker!

Chapter 4 Handling Disagreements on the Playground in Fifth Grade

```
W J T C E S S Q T M S H I V W T E L L J X X X
R I X F N U U R E Q G V A S R R X E S M K O Q
I M H M O X X X M A Z B T O C S J N L N F E O
F D D N Y S D O B X S R F Y M V Z V G O Q Y P
C O M P R O M I S E A L I D Y W G T Z K R B I
J N E Y E V O N K T E O N L R E C U S P W V N
W E E Z V R J I E L O U J C R M H V Y L J Z I
S K Y K E G T G H C O M U W Y T W K E E Z H O
P V O C Z D I Q R R Y L T I B A R X Q T E L N
W Z E R T E W E G Y A A E K K E A X B L H D P
C S E T S O A Y N F R A W D K C H Z N Q P D M
S X W N I T A K Q U S N L A O G U U F F Q M D
D U Q E I L N M L D P E M X K M I Q E Z B M C
B O D V P K V E E N P E L B N L L M M Y Y W O
S D E F S K S H X Y C A V D J G A X A I U T Q
P W D E F N M U L A M W D K X R A W C X Q X L
J V C Q O M A A E C A Y R Y B I S Y U S V E N
M K J H W L R P P W T F A B Y Q L O N N S P D
B Z K T L T P W E C U Z S P H S W I E M Q M D
R S N N U F Z U G U R V K G U H D B I O O Z Y
N A Z E K I L X N O I K J O J F E M B R S C Q
G A N Z L O O C Y A T S F A K G R I F F A O M
Z W U S N M O D V E Y D Z Q Z X J K K E S C W
```

compromise
creative
everyone
maturity
model

neutral
opinion
peacemaker
playground
recess

role
rules
staycool (stay cool)
strategies
walkaway

Chapter 5

How to Ask the Right Questions in Fifth Grade

Hey, fifth-grade thinker! Asking questions is like opening a treasure chest—you never know what amazing answers or ideas you'll discover. In fifth grade, your questions can take your learning to the next level. You're not just asking basic stuff anymore; now you're digging deeper, connecting ideas, and showing off your curiosity. But how do you ask the right questions? Don't worry, this chapter is packed with tips, strategies, and real-life scenarios to help you master the art of questioning. Let's dive in!

1. Know Why You're Asking
Before raising your hand, think about why you're asking. Are you trying to understand something better? Solving a problem? Get more details? Knowing your purpose will help you ask smarter questions.

Real-Life Scenario:
You're learning about the Revolutionary War, and your teacher says, "The colonies were unhappy with British taxes." Instead of asking, "What does that mean?" you ask, "What kinds of taxes were they paying, and how did it affect their lives?" Now you're getting a clearer picture and impressing your teacher with your thoughtfulness.

2. Build on What You Already Know
In fifth grade, your questions can connect what you've already learned to new information. This shows that you're paying attention and thinking critically.

Real-Life Scenario:
You're studying ecosystems and learned about food chains last year. When your teacher talks about predators, you ask, "How do predators affect the balance of the ecosystem?" You're connecting ideas and taking the discussion to a deeper level.

3. Ask Open-Ended Questions
Open-ended questions encourage discussion and longer answers. These often start with "why," "how," or "what." Steer clear of asking questions that can be answered with just "yes" or "no."

Real-Life Scenario:
In a math lesson, instead of asking, "Is this the right way to solve the problem?" you ask, "How can I check my work to make sure I solved this correctly?" This kind of question helps you understand the process, not just the answer.

4. Be Specific
Vague questions can confuse your teacher or classmates. Be clear about what you're asking to get the best possible answer.

Real-Life Scenario:
You're working on a science experiment, and your plant isn't growing. Instead of asking, "Why isn't this working?" you say, "Could the amount of sunlight or water I'm giving the plant be the problem?" Now your teacher knows exactly how to help.

5. Ask About Real-Life Connections
One of the coolest things about fifth grade is seeing how what you're learning connects to the real world. Ask questions that make those connections.

Real-Life Scenario:
You're learning about fractions and ask, "How do bakers use fractions when they're making recipes?" Your teacher gives an example of measuring ingredients, and suddenly fractions feel a lot more useful (and delicious).

6. Use Follow-Up Questions
Don't stop with just one question—ask follow-ups to dig deeper. This keeps the conversation going and helps you learn even more.

Real-Life Scenario:
During a history lesson, you ask, "Why did explorers risk their lives to travel to new places?" After your teacher answers, you follow up with, "How did their discoveries change the world?" Now you're learning about both the risks and the rewards.

7. Don't Be Afraid of Tough Topics
Sometimes, the best questions come from things you don't understand or find challenging. Don't be shy—tough questions often lead to the most interesting answers.

Real-Life Scenario:
In a lesson about gravity, you ask, "If gravity pulls everything down, how do airplanes stay in the air?" Your teacher explains lift and thrust, and now you're one step closer to understanding physics.

8. Ask Questions That Help the Whole Class

If you notice that other students look confused, ask a question that can help everyone. Your classmates will appreciate it, and your teacher will notice your leadership.

Real-Life Scenario:

Your teacher explains a new project, but some kids look unsure. You ask, "Can you give us an example of what the final project should look like?" The teacher shows a sample, and now everyone knows what to do.

9. Practice Active Listening

Good questions come from good listening. Pay attention to what your teacher and classmates are saying, you might come up with a great question based on their answers.

Real-Life Scenario:

During a group discussion, a classmate mentions that they think renewable energy is the future. You ask, "What makes renewable energy better than non-renewable energy?" Your question gets the whole group talking.

10. Turn Mistakes Into Questions

Mistakes are a normal part of learning. When you get something wrong, turn it into a question to figure out what happened.

Real-Life Scenario:

You get a math problem wrong and ask, "Can you show me where I went off track?" Your teacher explains the mistake, and you learn a new strategy for solving similar problems.

11. Use Technology to Ask Smarter Questions
Sometimes, technology can help you come up with great questions. Use online resources to learn a little more about a topic before asking something deeper in class.

Real-Life Scenario:
You're studying weather patterns and watching a video about hurricanes at home. The next day, you ask, "How do scientists predict when a hurricane will form?" Your question shows you've done extra research and are curious about the topic.

12. Write Down Your Questions
Sometimes, you think of a great question but forget it before you can ask. Keep a notebook or sticky notes handy to jot down questions during class.

Real-Life Scenario:
While reading about the Civil War, you wonder, "How did soldiers communicate during battles?" You write it in your notebook and ask during the next lesson. Your teacher gives a fascinating answer about signal flags and messengers.

13. Be Confident When Asking
It's okay to feel nervous about asking questions, but remember: your curiosity helps everyone learn. Speak clearly and confidently when it's your turn.

Real-Life Scenario:
You're unsure about how to start your book report and feel shy about asking. But when you finally ask, "What's the best way to write a strong introduction?" Your teacher gives helpful advice, and your report turns out great.

Final Thought

Asking the right questions in fifth grade is like unlocking secret doors to understanding. Whether you're curious about science, math, history, or just life in general, your questions show that you're engaged and ready to learn. Remember, the smartest people in the world are the ones who never stop asking questions. So, raise that hand, let your curiosity shine, and keep exploring the world one question at a time. You've got this, fifth-grade genius!

Chapter 5 How to Ask the Right Questions in Fifth Grade

```
E C U F E A X O J X H M V I H J K H D W R H D
N J G T G I Y B Z K U M E E B T A P F B I J W
N S Q P O I J B H O L V P E K O R Z R Q L H X
G H R I E D K T D S O W F P L E E S L V F K Z
R C U D I M Q J O N P I A M H C Y N Y G A Y R
T L G H S I N T O O E K S G Q K S O L G X H H
P G G F Q S X Q T I N K M T J B S I Z C S C T
A C C F M T G L N T E T F D H P V T R H F B W
B E O D S A E S E S N B Q H E D U C L A K V W
D R B X B K X I D E D O T C P Y A E T L S U K
T W I B E E H D I U E T I O K Z D N L L P O T
H O W C N S J A F Q D F P T K E C N J E X H C
D U F H J A U T N T I M Z F A C O O Z N G I I
Y A G L O V N S O C Z Y B A M M U C M G X Q U
M S G X H L W T C A G S H V R N R R I C Y I
Z O N N D R E C E X I O M T D W C O Z N Q Y D
O J I H R N A L X K T R C E L R O H F G S B X
B X N K R T Y A V M F F R Q W I B K H N I S T
Z V E E J J X S B H K S W C H T Z R A L I W C
P F T F J D G S B V T T F O A E C M Z U O P E
K L S I X R J M K A B M H B N W Y Y M A R B Y
G U I G A Q M A N P X M J V F O L L O W U P W
Q R L V D B G D S A W T E C H N O L O G Y W M
```

challenging
class
confident
connections
followup (follow up)

information
listening
mistakes
openended (open ended)
questions

specific
technology
understand
whole
write

Chapter 6

How to Rock Small Group Work in Fifth Grade

Hey there, teamwork expert! In fifth grade, working in small groups is a big part of your classroom experience. Whether you're tackling a science experiment, creating a history presentation, or solving a tricky math problem, you'll spend a lot of time collaborating with classmates. But let's be real working in groups can sometimes feel messy. People might have different ideas, or someone might not pull their weight. Don't worry! This chapter is packed with tips, real-life fifth-grade scenarios, and ideas to help you become a small-group superstar.

1. Start with a Group Plan
Before diving into your task, take a few minutes to come up with a game plan. Decide what the goal is, who's doing what, and how much time you have. A solid plan keeps everyone on track.

Real-Life Scenario:
Your group is building a model of the solar system. Instead of everyone grabbing random materials, you agree that one person will research the planets, another will gather materials, and someone else will design the layout. With a clear plan, your group finishes faster and better.

2. Respect Everyone's Ideas
In fifth grade, everyone's ideas matter—even if they're different from yours. Listen to what your teammates have to say and try to include their ideas in the project.

Real-Life Scenario:
Your group is brainstorming ideas for a class skit about historical explorers. One teammate suggests a comedy, while you're thinking of something serious. Instead of dismissing their idea, you say, "What if we make it funny but also include the important facts?" Now everyone's happy, and your skit stands out.

3. Divide the Work Fairly
No one likes being in a group where one person does all the work. Make sure everyone has a job and that the workload is shared evenly.

Real-Life Scenario:
You're creating a poster about the food chain. You say, "I'll draw the pictures, and you can write the facts. Does someone want to make the title?" By dividing tasks, your group works efficiently, and no one feels left out.

4. Speak Up (But Stay Polite)
If something isn't working, don't stay quiet. Speak up—but do it respectfully. Pointing out problems in a kind way helps your group improve without causing arguments.

Real-Life Scenario:
One group member is doodling instead of working on the project. You say, "Hey, we could really use your help with this section. Can you work on the diagram while we finish the text?" They refocus and start contributing.

5. Use Your Strengths
Everyone in the group has something they're good at. Play to your strengths and let others use theirs. This makes the project stronger and more fun.

Real-Life Scenario:
You're great at presenting, but not so much at drawing. Another teammate loves art. You suggest, "Why don't you handle the visuals while I work on practicing the presentation?" By splitting the work this way, you both shine.

6. Be Patient with Differences
Not everyone works the same way. Some people are super-fast, while others take their time. Be patient and focus on getting the job done together.

Real-Life Scenario:
Your group is solving a math problem, and one teammate is slower at calculations. Instead of getting frustrated, you say, "Take your time. Let's double-check it together to make sure it's right." Now they feel supported, and your group stays on track.

7. Handle Disagreements Calmly
It's normal to have disagreements in a group. What matters is how you handle them. Stay calm, listen to each other, and work toward a solution.

Real-Life Scenario:
Your group is deciding what colors to use for a project. Two people want blue, and two want green. You suggest, "Why don't we use both? Blue for the title and green for the details." Problem solved, and everyone's happy.

8. Keep an Eye on the Time
Projects often come with deadlines. Keep track of how much time you have left and make sure your group stays focused.

Real-Life Scenario:
You're working on a science experiment and realize there are only ten minutes left. You say, "Let's finish the last step quickly and save time to clean up." Your group listens, and you finish just in time.

9. Encouragement
Encouragement goes a long way. If someone is struggling or feeling unsure, cheer them on and remind them of their strengths.

Real-Life Scenario:
Your teammate is nervous about presenting in front of the class. You say, "You've got this! Your part about the rainforest is so interesting—I know the class will love it." They smile, and their confidence grows.

10. Take Responsibility
If something goes wrong, don't point fingers. Take responsibility for your part and work together to fix it.

Real-Life Scenario:
Your group forgets to include an important fact in your presentation. Instead of blaming each other, you say, "Let's add it to the Q&A at the end so we can still share the information." Your teamwork saves the day.

11. Celebrate Your Success
When your group finishes a project, take a moment to celebrate what you've accomplished. High-five each other, say "good job," and feel proud of your teamwork.

Real-Life Scenario:
Your group presents a model of a volcano, and the class loves it. Afterward, you say, "Great job, everyone! The lava effect was amazing." Your teammates smile, and you all feel proud of what you created together.

Final Thought
Working in small groups in fifth grade is about more than just finishing a project—it's about learning how to listen, share ideas, and support each other. By staying organized, respecting your teammates, and keeping a positive attitude, you can make group work not just successful but fun too. So, the next time your teacher says, "Find a partner or group," don't stress—use these tips, dive in, and show everyone how a fifth-grade teamwork superstar gets it done. You've got this!

Chapter 6 How to Rock Small Group Work in Fifth Grade

```
G G U I B L T D S W S W C D E X L P F P N D G
Y G N A L P S I D H R O T E Z Y Q D Z X N Q K
R R Q J I A M G I Y Y R D A Y B E C T V Q I E
T O Z F E F A V X M T I R I A Z V I W E O L M
T U U D H B C V C D V J T I M X I W U T B K H
T P I Z C Z N M V I R X E M B A E E A N E R T
N S C R V R T O D U I B P D O Q A P B O U R N
F I X P T T C N S E C N E R E F F I D P Q I U
A Z B Q P D E Y O B S F H F F O C U S E D S D
I X F R L F P R J Z V J M P Y J Y E Q N W U K
R K K E Q T S N S Q X O V N J A T X V Z B Z M
L Z U S M N E Q D A S T R E N G T H S E H U F
Y C T P O E R P E D B F L G L N X V Y S P F C
P R F O O M L S D T B C K J F E N I R I T I U
S F N N R E Q D Q V Z A W E E A X V S P F R K
D S V S S G F B C Y W L Z G D W K F F S S Z H
I Y A I S A R A K D W M L X V J R H N P Q H B
X P D B A R X X I K V L L S V D U Z E O P R C
U M D I L U S V O G N Y B F J F M A F M A C H
R Q T L C O I E H I D J M P H T K M V K C R C
M W A I X C E F V A F I F P M U T E J J Q Z R
F E O T P N W N V M E S V F P O G D F B I P M
P D S Y E E W S M A L L A S S N X N Y W R T D
```

calmly	fairly	respect
classroom	focused	responsibility
differences	groups	small
divide	ideas	speakup (speak up)
encouragement	plan	strengths

Chapter 7

How to Succeed in Studying History in Fifth Grade

Hey there, history explorer! Fifth grade is a big step up when it comes to history. You'll learn about major events, important people, and how the past shapes our lives today. But history isn't just about memorizing dates and facts—it's about discovering stories, making connections, and understanding why things happened the way they did. In this chapter, you'll find tons of tips, real-life fifth-grade scenarios, and ideas to help you rock your history lessons. Ready to dig into the past and uncover its secrets? Let's go!

1. Understand the "Why" Behind the Facts
In fifth grade, history isn't just about knowing what happened—it's about understanding why it happened. When you learn a new topic, ask yourself: Why did people make these choices? What were they trying to achieve?

Real-Life Scenario:
Your class is learning about the American Revolution. Instead of just memorizing the date of the Boston Tea Party, you ask, "Why did the colonists throw tea into the harbor?" You learn it was a protest against unfair taxes, and suddenly, it all makes sense.

2. Make History Personal
History feels more real when you connect it to your own life or interests. Think about how events from the past relate to things you care about today.

Real-Life Scenario:
You love skateboarding, and your teacher mentions the industrial revolution made transportation faster and easier. You wonder, "Would skateboards have been possible without all those changes?" Connecting history to something you love makes it stick in your mind.

3. Use Timelines to See the Big Picture
Timelines are like maps that help you see how historical events connect. Creating a timeline for what you're learning can help you keep track of events in order.

Real-Life Scenario:
Your class is studying the Civil War. You make a timeline starting with Abraham Lincoln's election in 1860 and ending with the war's conclusion in 1865. Seeing the events in order helps you understand how everything unfolded.

4. Dive Into Primary Sources
Primary sources—like letters, diaries, or old photographs—are like time machines that take you straight to the past. They show you how people really thought and felt at the time.

Real-Life Scenario:
Your teacher shows you a diary entry from a soldier during the Civil War. You read about his daily struggles, and it helps you understand the war from a personal perspective. It's like meeting someone from history face-to-face!

5. Turn History Into a Story
History is full of amazing stories and treating it like one can make it more fun and easier to remember. Think of the people in history as characters and the events as parts of a big adventure.

Real-Life Scenario:
When studying explorers like Christopher Columbus, imagine you're reading an adventure book. Picture Columbus sailing across the ocean, battling storms, and discovering new lands. Suddenly, his journey feels exciting, not boring.

6. Watch Documentaries or Videos
Sometimes, seeing history come to life on screen can help you understand it better. Look for age-appropriate videos or documentaries about the topics you're studying.

Real-Life Scenario:
You're learning about ancient Egypt, and your teacher shows a video about how the pyramids were built. Watching workers move massive stones with simple tools helps you realize how incredible those structures are.

7. Ask Questions to Dig Deeper
Good historians ask lots of questions. Don't stop at just learning the basics—dig deeper by asking "why," "how," or "what if" questions.

Real-Life Scenario:
You're studying the Great Depression and wonder, "How did families survive without much money?" Your teacher explains how people traded goods and grew their own food. You even research how those struggles led to changes in the economy.

8. Join Group Discussions
Talking about history with your classmates helps you hear different perspectives and learn new ideas. Sharing your thoughts and listen to others—it's a win-win.

Real-Life Scenario:
During a discussion about women's suffrage, a classmate points out that some women faced even more challenges because of their race. You realize history isn't just one story—it's made up of many experiences.

9. Practice Writing Like a Historian
In fifth grade, you'll write essays or reports about history. Start by organizing your ideas, backing them up with evidence, and making your writing clear and detailed.

Real-Life Scenario:
You're writing a report about the Louisiana Purchase. Instead of just saying, "It was big," you write, "The Louisiana Purchase doubled the size of the United States and allowed settlers to move west." Adding facts makes your report stronger and more impressive.

10. Relate History to Current Events
History doesn't just stay in the past—it connects to things happening today. Look for ways to relate what you're learning to current events or issues.

Real-Life Scenario:
You're studying immigration in the early 1900s and thinking about how people move to new places today. You ask your teacher, "What are the biggest reasons people immigrate now compared to back then?" It helps you see history as part of a bigger story.

11. Turn Studying Into a Game
Make history fun by turning it into a game. Use flashcards, trivia quizzes, or even role-playing to make studying more exciting.

Real-Life Scenario:
You and a friend quiz each other on Revolutionary War facts. They ask, "Who wrote the Declaration of Independence?" You answer, "Thomas Jefferson!" It feels more like a game than homework, and you both learn faster.

12. Visit Historical Sites or Museums
If you can, visit places connected to the history you're studying. Seeing artifacts or standing where events happened makes history come alive.

Real-Life Scenario:
Your class takes a trip to a local museum with an exhibit on Native American history. You see tools, clothing, and artwork from hundreds of years ago, and it makes the lessons from class feel real and exciting.

13. Use Creative Tools
Try using drawings, charts, or even comics to explain historical events. These visual tools help you understand and remember what you've learned.

Real-Life Scenario:
You create a comic strip showing Paul Revere's midnight ride. Drawing the events helps you understand the story and makes studying way more fun.

Final Thought

Studying history in fifth grade is about more than just facts—it's about discovering the amazing stories of the past and understanding how they shape the world today. By asking questions, making connections, and using these strategies, you'll not only succeed in history class but also find yourself enjoying the journey through time. So grab your notebook, put on your explorer hat, and dive into the incredible adventure of history. You've got this, historian-in-the-making!

Chapter 7 How to Succeed in Studying History in Fifth Grade

```
Y T Y Z P L J W W I J W F W O F Y C Z O D J C
J U I Z L P C M P Q A Z Z I C W P R S I H F R
Q G S T G V G P L T A C T J A Z C V O M K C E
Q Z T N N B I H N R I P K L L G D C I T U C S
D O C U M E N T A R I E S E F T G Y E R S N S
M W A F Q O D B F T I G Q W W U J A R O E I H
A Q F R I O B L P Z T L A X S C W E L G C V H
J S X C Y Y S U B K J Z Q I I J N W D P R M B
V B Q H H L S R T M Y L I V W T Y S I J U O Z
R L L M X U U H W V Q A M M V H F G P I O T H
Y T K F T G T V S P O U C U B I D X P J S I X
L J O I L Q S A D M K F E K V E D O D U Q M G
R C S I U R A U A V G M H S R P E E J F A E O
K I Y G N L W W C V K A L G T P F V O L P L H
V B H H B H L U C L N A P J H I N I E S M I Q
U K P T W A Z S V E J G Y N E H O N U N D N S
H D I S C U S S I O N S I C Z U A N M G T E L
U W A C E C I T C A R P O H T E U F S P O S T
C B A J H I N H C U I P W A T D W N Z V X N B
A P R X T G U G C J L J M G G T C T O C S Z Q
P R I M A R Y V T H I N Y S O C U K R O N Y O
C S I L O O B V K X V O R N D T A C Y A H D C
L A N O S R E P Z K A Y V Y R O T S H X R W H
```

current	history	sources
discussions	personal	story
documentaries	practice	timelines
events	primary	videos
facts	questions	visit

Chapter 8

How to Master Fifth Grade Math

Hey there, math whiz! Fifth grade math is a whole new adventure. You'll dive into big topics like fractions, decimals, geometry, and even some algebra-like thinking. It might feel a little challenging at times, but guess what? You've got what it takes to conquer it. This chapter is packed with tips, real-life fifth-grade scenarios, and ideas to help you succeed. Let's get those pencils sharpened and math brains fired up—your best math year yet starts now!

1. Understand the "Why" Behind the Math
In fifth grade, math isn't just about getting the answer—it's about understanding how and why it works. When you understand the "why," you can tackle tougher problems with confidence.

Real-Life Scenario:
You're learning about fractions, and your teacher explains that 3/4 and 6/8 are equivalent fractions. Instead of just memorizing it, you ask, "Why are they the same?" Your teacher shows you how multiplying both the numerator and denominator by 2 keeps the value the same. Now it clicks, and you feel ready for any fraction challenge.

2. Use Real-Life Math
Math isn't just for class—it's everywhere! Look for ways to use math in your daily life, whether it's cooking, shopping, or playing games.

Real-Life Scenario:
You're at a pizza party and someone asks, "If we cut each pizza into 8 slices, how many slices will we have from 3 pizzas?" You quickly multiply 8 × 3 and answer, "24 slices!" Everyone's impressed, and you realize how useful multiplication really is.

3. Break Down Big Problems

Fifth-grade math problems can sometimes feel overwhelming, especially word problems. The trick is to break them into smaller steps and tackle them one at a time.

Real-Life Scenario:

A problem says: "A library has 300 books. If 1/5 of the books are science books, how many are science books?" You break it down:

Step 1: Divide 300 by 5.
Step 2: Realize the answer is 60.
Now you know there are 60 science books without feeling stuck.

4. Master Your Multiplication and Division Facts

If you know your multiplication and division facts like the back of your hand, everything else—fractions, decimals, and even geometry—gets easier.

Real-Life Scenario:

You're solving a long division problem, 672 ÷ 8. Because you've practiced your multiplication facts, you know that 8 × 84 = 672 without a calculator. Your teacher gives you a thumbs-up for solving it quickly and correctly.

5. Use Visual Tools

Math can be tricky when it's all numbers on a page. Visual tools like number lines, fraction strips, or diagrams can help you see the problem in a new way.

Real-Life Scenario:
You're comparing 0.25 and 1/4 to see if they're the same. Using a fraction strip and a decimal number line, you realize they both represent the same value. Suddenly, decimals and fractions don't seem so different anymore!

6. Check Your Work
Even math geniuses make mistakes, but checking your work can save you. Take a few extra minutes to review your steps and see if your answer makes sense.

Real-Life Scenario:
You solve a problem and get 7.5 as your answer. You go back to the question, which asks how many whole pizzas are needed for a party. Realizing your mistake, you round up to 8 pizzas—it wouldn't make sense to serve half a pizza at a party!

7. Ask Questions When You're Stuck
If you don't understand something, don't be afraid to ask your teacher or a classmate for help. Asking questions shows that you're paying attention and want to learn.

Real-Life Scenario:
You're struggling to figure out how to convert fractions to decimals. You ask your teacher, "Why does dividing the numerator by the denominator work?" They explain it step by step, and now you're confident for the next quiz.

8. Practice, Practice, Practice

Math is like riding a bike—the more you practice, the better you get. Spend a few extra minutes each day reviewing what you learned in class.

Real-Life Scenario:

Your teacher gives you a worksheet on adding decimals. Instead of rushing through it, you take your time to make sure each decimal point is lined up. By the end, you've nailed every question and feel great about decimals.

9. Turn Mistakes Into Learning Opportunities

Mistakes aren't failures, they're opportunities to learn. When you get something wrong, figure out what happened and try again.

Real-Life Scenario:

You mix up perimeter and area on a geometry test. Instead of feeling frustrated, you review the definitions: perimeter is the distance around, and area is the space inside. Next time, you nail both concepts!

10. Challenge Yourself

Once you've mastered the basics, try solving more challenging problems. This keeps math exciting and helps you grow your skills.

Real-Life Scenario:

Your teacher gives you a bonus question: "If you travel 60 miles in 2 hours, how far will you go in 5 hours at the same speed?" You realize you need to multiply 60 by 2.5 and solve it step by step. Your teacher is impressed with your problem-solving skills!

11. Use Online Tools and Apps
There are tons of fun apps and websites that make math feel like a game. Use them to practice and explore new concepts.

Real-Life Scenario:
You download an app that lets you practice fractions with fun challenges. After playing for just 15 minutes a day, you notice that fractions feel way easier during class.

12. Work With a Friend
Sometimes, working with a classmate can help you understand math better. You can explain things to each other and learn together.

Real-Life Scenario:
You and a friend pair up to solve a tricky math puzzle. They notice a mistake in your equation, and you help them understand how to set up the problem. Together, you crack the puzzle and high-five in victory!

13. Celebrate Your Progress
Math isn't always easy, so celebrate your wins—big or small. When you master a new concept or improve your test score, take a moment to feel proud.

Real-Life Scenario:
You finally figure out how to solve multi-step word problems, and your teacher gives you a shout-out in class. You feel proud and motivated to tackle even more challenges.

Final Thought

Fifth grade math might seem tough at first, but with curiosity, practice, and a little patience, you can master it. Remember, math isn't about being perfect, it's about learning, growing, and finding the best way to solve problems. So, grab your pencil, dive into those numbers, and show fifth-grade math who's boss. Let's go!

Chapter 8 How to Master Fifth Grade Math

```
R S X F A T P J D C S U N B O O F N K K U N X
C O S C I N B F V O U E Z X Q Y I P M I W V R
R K M P Y S X D D U M J R Q I H Q E P C K E J
D N W L P L Q T Q M E B V U F A A C H H A K D
H T N E Q T Y G W X G I Y R O D B A X L D I H
F J T H J R J Q H L S C A S Y M L H L V G F E
W S M V I V S N U U A C E G Z L D I U F Q D R
E V S I C T H J A R T Y D W E U F W C J B E B
S M B D S B W L I I M P W N R E R G I U R Q L
Q H I Y I T Z V O S R W G Q F X W V U N T J O
C U R U P I A N N Q I E D T I T V J S S R O X
W A E N V V S K I N A Y R T E M O E G D Q R T
O E C S H T Y F E L D E C I M A L S V C C V O
L B B G T L Y I Q S G T E C S Y W I J K E G O
O W I S W I E K F N P L U U Y B H G C G N M L
C C C N I P O S E P S P O A P E R E L L A M S
I D X H E T J N O B H U K W T V I K M R R R D
C M H G B Y E T S P K T K M D G M R K R I W L
N K Q X L J T S T W C D C R W T Q A M D D Z T
L T H N T Q Y A D I P P E D B Q W H T C W F Y
C S W P Z O N K A E J T H G F J P L Q H A S V
G Y E T L D Z T O U P W C D N A T S R E D N U
F H F L Z X V Z Y J Y B L O L H Z N B Q D Y E
```

challenge   math   steps
check   mistakes   tools
decimals   questions   understand
fractions   reallife (real life) visual
geometry   smaller   websites

Chapter 9

How to Succeed in Reading in Fifth Grade

Hey there, bookworm! Fifth grade is an exciting year for readers. This is the year where you dive into longer books, more challenging texts, and stories with deeper themes. But reading isn't just about finishing books, it's about understanding what you read, making connections, and discovering how stories can change the way you see the world. Whether you're already a book lover or just learning to enjoy reading, this chapter will give you tons of tips and real-life fifth-grade scenarios to help you become a reading superstar. Let's turn the page and get started!

1. Read With a Purpose
In fifth grade, you'll read for all kinds of reasons: to learn, to prepare for discussions, or just for fun. Knowing why you're reading helps you stay focused and get the most out of it.

Real-Life Scenario:
Your teacher assigns a chapter from a history book about the Civil War. Instead of just reading the words, you ask yourself, "What am I supposed to learn from this?" You highlight key dates and events, and when your teacher asks questions in class, you're ready to answer.

2. Explore Different Genres
Fifth grade is the perfect time to step out of your comfort zone and explore new genres like historical fiction, biographies, poetry, or even science fiction. Each genre teaches you something different.

Real-Life Scenario:
You've always loved adventure stories, but your teacher recommends a historical fiction book about kids during World War II. At first, you're unsure, but as you read, you realize the story is just as exciting as your favorite adventures—and you're learning about history, too.

3. Take Notes While You Read
Keeping a notebook or sticky notes nearby can help you track important ideas, words you don't know, or things you want to remember. This makes it easier to discuss or write about the book later.

Real-Life Scenario:
You're reading a mystery novel, and the detective keeps mentioning a strange blue key. You jot down, "Blue key—important?" Later, when the key unlocks the final clue, you feel like a detective yourself!

4. Make Predictions
Good readers don't just follow the story, they try to guess what will happen next. Making predictions keeps you engaged and helps you think critically about the plot.

Real-Life Scenario:
In a fantasy book, the main character finds a mysterious map. You predict, "This map will lead them to treasure, but there will be traps along the way." As you read, you check to see if your prediction was right.

5. Ask Questions While You Read

Great readers are curious. As you read, ask questions like, "Why is this happening? What will the character do next? How does this connect to the bigger story?" This keeps your brain active and makes reading more fun.

Real-Life Scenario:
In a book about explorers, you wonder, "How did they survive without modern technology?" Your curiosity leads you to look up more about survival skills, and you end up writing a cool extra credit report for class.

6. Visualize the Story

Close your eyes and picture what's happening in the book. Imagine the characters, the setting, and the action like a movie playing in your head. Visualization helps you stay focused and remember the details.

Real-Life Scenario:
You're reading a book about a shipwreck, and you imagine the roaring waves, the broken sails, and the characters clinging to a lifeboat. When your teacher asks about the setting, you describe it like you were really there.

7. Pay Attention to Themes

In fifth grade, books often have deeper themes, like bravery, friendship, or standing up for what's right. Think about what the book is trying to teach you and how it connects to your life.

Real-Life Scenario:
In a story about a girl helping her community after a hurricane, you realize the theme is about teamwork and kindness. It makes you think about how you can help others in your own neighborhood.

8. Discuss What You Read

Talking about books with your classmates, family, or friends can help you understand them better and hear different perspectives. Plus, it's fun to share your favorite parts!

Real-Life Scenario:

Your class reads a book about space travel, and during a group discussion, a classmate points out something you didn't notice: the main character's fear of failure. You realize it's a big part of the story, and now you see the book in a whole new way.

9. Build Your Vocabulary

Fifth-grade books often include challenging words. When you find a word, you don't know, try using context clues or looking it up. Then, practice using it in your own writing or conversations.

Real-Life Scenario:

You come across the word perseverance in a story about an inventor. After looking it up, you use it in a sentence during your next class discussion: "The character showed perseverance by never giving up on their invention."

10. Reread When Needed

If a part of the book doesn't make sense, don't be afraid to go back and reread it. Sometimes, you'll notice details you missed the first time.

Real-Life Scenario:

You're confused about why a character made a certain decision. You reread the previous chapter and find a hint you missed—a letter they received explaining their plan. Now the story makes more sense.

11. Set Reading Goals
Challenge yourself to read a certain number of books, explore new genres, or tackle a longer novel this year. Setting goals helps you stay motivated and focused.

Real-Life Scenario:
You set a goal to read three biographies this semester. By the end of the term, you've learned about Abraham Lincoln, Marie Curie, and Harriet Tubman—and you feel inspired by their amazing stories.

12. Use Technology to Your Advantage
Audiobooks, e-readers, and online resources can make reading more accessible and fun. Use them to explore new stories and learn in different ways.

Real-Life Scenario:
You listen to an audiobook of The Secret Garden while riding in the car. Hearing the voices and sound effects brings the story to life, and you can't wait to discuss it in class.

Final Thought
Reading in fifth grade isn't just about finishing books—it's about exploring new worlds, learning big ideas, and growing as a thinker. By trying new genres, asking questions, and discussing what you read, you'll become a stronger reader and discover stories that stay with you forever. So, grab a book, find a cozy spot, and dive into your next reading adventure. You've got this, fifth-grade reader!

Chapter 9 How to Succeed in Reading in Fifth Grade

```
W G P Z O S F B A O Q Y W J G R M H B T R Z C
Q B O X R L N R I V U I P C K I H H D W I W I
P K P Y J A E A N O R E U Q H R V A M K H H Y
L V J T R O D U X C B O R W Z C L Q C Q U H Y
E D N S B G A C A P F U P L O Z P G G A G O B
E N D G E P E G V D N H O T N O T E S I E Q Q
C J N D R M R W Y X J Q S C P A C Q C O N W N
C Y B V Z P E E A H X A E U W Y S H M T R L B
I S E F C L R H D U F D G A S I J B I I E Y Z
Z R Z A S F D U T I Q M Y Q S Y J Q O R S Y I
A Q I U F S D V B R C I X E J L E G J P H H V
C U L D T Y Y Q T Z W T J F L X T A L I E P O
L E A I S L D Q J Y E Y I N P B O W D M C S H
M S U O B H X D G A H X U O M A N C L E I M N
Q T S B O O K W O R M D P J N Q M K A V K E V
X I I O I A T K E B K H Y L B S Q O I Q A J V
H O V O R K F A S N D U Z N O P L H O R V R L
R N V K O X D D S J V X M R Z R T X D E D B A
X S N S V I M T U I C S T P H K E P Z E N E J
K N P U N J T C E A B C M B T H U Q B U U L Y
I I D G Y R A L U B A C O V Z K C X N K R G N
F R L B Q N C W K S H L D S J D C I U V V P O
E S S U C S I D Z P L C I D E T L G Z S W E I
```

audiobooks	goals	reading
bookworm	notes	reread
discuss	predictions	themes
explore	purpose	visualize
genres	questions	vocabulary

Chapter 10
How to Succeed in Fifth Grade P.E.

Hey there, future athlete! Fifth grade physical education (P.E.) is about more than just running laps or playing games. It's your chance to build skills, improve your fitness, and learn how to be a leader and teammate. You'll face new challenges, but you'll also have more opportunities to shine. Whether you're a sports pro or just in it for fun, this chapter is packed with tips, ideas, and real-life scenarios to help you crush it in P.E. class. Let's get moving!

1. Set Personal Fitness Goals
By fifth grade, you're ready to start setting goals for yourself in P.E. Maybe you want to run faster, improve your jump shot, or do more push-ups. Goals give you something to work toward and help you see how much you're improving.

Real-Life Scenario:
You're not great at pull-ups, and during the first fitness test, you can only do one. Instead of feeling down, you set a goal to do five by the end of the semester. Every week, you practice, and when the next test comes around, you hit your goal. That's progress!

2. Step Out of Your Comfort Zone
Fifth grade P.E. might include activities you've never tried before, like volleyball, yoga, or even a dance routine. Don't be afraid to give new things a shot—you might discover a hidden talent or a new favorite sport.

Real-Life Scenario:
Your class starts learning how to juggle scarves, and at first, you think, "This is so weird!" But after a few tries, you realize it's actually fun. By the end of the unit, you're juggling like a pro and even showing your friends how to do it.

3. Be a Team Player
In fifth grade, teamwork becomes even more important. Whether you're playing soccer, basketball, or capture the flag, learning how to work with others is a skill that will help you both on and off the field.

Real-Life Scenario:
During a soccer game, your teammate has a clear shot at the goal, but they're nervous. You shout, "You've got this!" They take the shot, score, and thank you for the encouragement. Your teamwork helped your team win!

4. Learn the Rules of the Game
Every sport has its own rules and understanding them is key to playing well. When your teacher explains the rules, listen carefully—it makes the game more fun and less confusing.

Real-Life Scenario:
You're playing kickball and didn't realize you could tag someone out by throwing the ball. After learning the rule, you tag out two players in one inning. Knowing the rules makes you a stronger player!

5. Focus on Sportsmanship
Winning is great; but being a good sport matter more. Congratulate the other team when they win, shake hands after the game, and cheer on your teammates, even when things don't go your way.

Real-Life Scenario:
Your basketball team loses a close game, and you feel disappointed. Instead of pouting, you tell the other team, "Good game!" and high-five your teammates for their effort. Your positive attitude shows true sportsmanship.

6. Stay Active Outside of P.E.

The skills you learn in P.E. will improve even more if you stay active outside of class. Join a team, ride your bike, or play outside with friends to keep building strength and stamina.

Real-Life Scenario:
You start shooting hoops in your driveway every weekend, and by the time the basketball unit rolls around in P.E., your skills have improved so much that your teacher notices. Practice really does make perfect!

7. Practice Leadership Skills

Fifth grade is your time to step up as a leader. Offer to help explain drills to younger students or be a captain during team games. Leadership shows your teacher you're ready for bigger responsibilities.

Real-Life Scenario:
Your class is learning how to play volleyball, and some of your classmates are struggling to serve. You volunteer to show them the right form, and your teacher praises you for being a leader. Your classmates appreciate the help too!

8. Dress for Success

The right gear makes a big difference in P.E. Wear comfortable clothes and shoes that let you move easily. Bring a water bottle to stay hydrated, especially on hot days.

Real-Life Scenario:
You forget your sneakers one day and have to run laps in your boots. It's uncomfortable, and you can't keep up. After that, you make sure to check your bag the night before, so you're always prepared.

9. Learn to Solve Conflicts Fairly

Disagreements can happen during games, whether it's about a foul, a point, or who gets to go next. Learn to handle conflicts calmly and fairly so everyone can enjoy the game.

Real-Life Scenario:
Two players argue over whether the ball was in or out during a tennis game. Instead of taking sides, you suggest replaying the point. The game continues smoothly, and your classmates appreciate your fairness.

10. Celebrate Small Wins

Improvement takes time, so celebrate the small victories along the way. Maybe you ran one extra lap or hit the ball over the net for the first time—every step forward counts.

Real-Life Scenario:
You finally make contact with the ball in softball after missing several times. Your teammates cheer, and you feel proud of your progress, even though you didn't score a run. Small wins lead to big achievements!

11. Take Care of Your Body

P.E. can be demanding, so make sure to eat healthy foods, drink plenty of water, and get enough sleep. This keeps you energized and ready to perform your best.

Real-Life Scenario:
You skip breakfast one morning and feel sluggish during a running drill. The next day, you eat a banana and some toast, and you have enough energy to finish the drill strongly. Lesson learned!

12. Have Fun and Stay Positive

At the end of the day, P.E. is about enjoying yourself. Even if you're not the fastest runner or the strongest player, keep a positive attitude and have fun with your classmates.

Real-Life Scenario:
You're not great at dodgeball, but instead of focusing on getting out, you decide to cheer on your team from the sidelines. Your energy lifts everyone up, and you have just as much fun as if you were still in the game.

Final Thought
Fifth grade P.E. is your chance to grow stronger, build skills, and learn valuable lessons about teamwork and leadership. By staying active, trying new things, and keeping a positive attitude, you'll make the most of every class. So lace up your sneakers, grab that ball, and get ready to show everyone what you've got. You've got this, fifth-grade champion!

Chapter 10 How to Succeed in Fifth Grade P.E.

```
C R V L Y G K C T Q Y T Q E R L O Z H Y I G X
A L I R C S H R P F L A R M W G D L U D R V V
U X Z R Y Y S C O V M O E O E T Y B F B P J D
Y L F Q D M A U X W V H X F F C W W H M L P M
U B I R M F S I E F M E Z T R M I H W I O V M
R Z A O X X F Z O O R A Y Y Y F O G L B W G Z
Q T A X V G Q H O K I L E W R H E C L E M H S
E J O A D E G O H Z D T J T I L T P E H A L X
Y D B N T A H C I V B H J S P K P T O V L I B
Y Z F E R R I B W H V Y W B D F C M I I S U Y
I E U K L O W P E L O H X Q E B F L K P F Z X
F X Q D P A V T S P O R T S M A N S H I P U C
V W X H A U V B O V E S U T S D O O F V B L L
R N Z V C A E I B F G E T A R B E L E C I V J
L D W W T E W C K M F W Z V F F I T N E S S B
E W X G I H G C J K E F T R J H U O N Y C D A
W G G Y V D H B R M S H J A R W N S J R U N D
W V D Z E L O X Q Q A M Q N J S P L V X J Z J
C H S R C P H Y S I C A L E D U C A T I O N K
B E X S U L B T S D B C E M G F Q O R F P L T
F O L E F L K X N W B L V G A N O G X F B K G
I E O X S Z E Y A I C F F N F D B B I F S G H
Y Y H Q Q W W S W J Y L R I A F F C R P J C E
```

active	foods	physicaleducation
celebrate	gear	(physical education)
comfort	goals	rules
fairly	healthy	skills
fitness	hydrate	sportsmanship
		teamwork

Chapter 11
How to Succeed in Science in Fifth Grade

Hey there, future scientist! Fifth grade science is all about diving deeper into the wonders of the world. You'll study fascinating topics like ecosystems, energy, the solar system, and even how tiny cells work. But science isn't just about memorizing facts—it's about discovering, experimenting, and thinking like a real scientist. This chapter is packed with tips, real-life scenarios, and ideas to help you rock fifth-grade science. Let's grab our goggles, roll up our sleeves, and explore how to make science your new favorite subject!

1. Get Curious and Ask Big Questions
Science starts with curiosity. Wondering how something works or why it happens is the first step to learning. Don't just accept what's in your textbook—ask questions to dig deeper.

Real-Life Scenario:
Your teacher explains that plants use photosynthesis to make food. You wonder, "What happens to plants in the dark?" You ask your teacher, and they explain how plants store energy for nighttime. Your curiosity helps you learn something extra.

2. Experiment Like a Pro
In fifth grade, you'll do more hands-on experiments. Pay close attention to instructions, but don't be afraid to make predictions or try new ideas. Experimenting is how scientists make discoveries.

Real-Life Scenario:
Your class is testing how different materials affect ice melting. You predict that aluminum foil will keep the ice from melting quickly. After testing, you find out you're right, and your teacher calls it a "scientific win!"

3. Learn to Record Data

Great scientists keep detailed records. Use charts, graphs, or tables to organize your observations and results. Neat, accurate data makes it easier to analyze your findings.

Real-Life Scenario:
Your class is growing bean plants to see how sunlight affects growth. You measure the height of your plant every day and record it in a chart. When it's time to write your conclusion, your data shows that plants in sunlight grow twice as tall. Your chart makes your project shine.

4. Use Science Vocabulary

Fifth grade science introduces lots of new words, like ecosystem, evaporation, and energy transfer. Using these terms correctly shows that you understand the concepts.

Real-Life Scenario:
Your teacher asks, "What happens when water heats up?" Instead of saying, "It turns into steam," you say, "The water evaporates into water vapor." Your teacher nods, impressed by your use of science vocabulary.

5. Make Real-World Connections

Science isn't just for the classroom, it's everywhere! Look for ways to connect what you're learning to the world around you.

Real-Life Scenario:
You're studying simple machines, and you notice how a seesaw at the park works like a lever. When you tell your teacher, they smile and say, "Exactly! Science is all around us." Suddenly, simple machines feel much cooler.

6. Collaborate With Your Classmates
Many science projects in fifth grade involve group work. Share ideas, listen to others, and divide tasks to make teamwork successful.

Real-Life Scenario:
Your group is building a wind-powered car for a class project. One teammate designs the wheels, another works on the sail, and you test the car. By working together, you create the fastest car in the class.

7. Pay Attention to Patterns
In science, patterns often reveal important clues. Whether you're observing the phases of the moon or studying animal behavior, look for patterns to help you make discoveries.

Real-Life Scenario:
You're tracking the moon's shape every night for a month. After a week, you notice it's getting fuller and fuller. By the end of the month, you've seen a complete lunar cycle—and you understand how the phases repeat.

8. Use Technology to Explore
Science and technology go hand in hand. Use apps, videos, and simulations to dive deeper into topics and explore things you can't see in the classroom.

Real-Life Scenario:
You're learning about the solar system, and your teacher shows a virtual reality app that lets you explore the planets. Flying around Jupiter and Saturn makes the lesson unforgettable.

9. Practice Critical Thinking

Science is about asking questions, testing ideas, and analyzing results. Think critically about what you observe and why it happens.

Real-Life Scenario:
Your experiment shows that saltwater freezes slower than fresh water. Instead of just writing the result, you ask, "Why does salt slow freezing?" After some research, you find out that salt lowers the freezing point. You've just taken your understanding to the next level!

10. Stay Organized

Science often involves multiple steps, like forming a hypothesis, collecting data, and writing a conclusion. Keeping your materials and notes organized will make the process easier.

Real-Life Scenario:
You're doing a science fair project about how different liquids affect plant growth. By organizing your notes, photos, and data charts in a binder, you impress the judges and feel confident presenting your project.

11. Accept That Mistakes Are Part of Learning

Not every experiment will go perfectly, and that's okay. Mistakes are part of science—they help you learn what doesn't work so you can find out what does.

Real-Life Scenario:
You're testing how baking soda and vinegar react, but your measurements are off, and nothing happens. Instead of getting upset, you try again with the correct amounts. This time, your experiment creates the best volcano eruption in class!

12. Share What You Learn
Great scientists communicate their findings. Whether it's through a presentation, report, or class discussion, share your discoveries with others.

Real-Life Scenario:
Your group learns that certain colors absorb more heat than others. During your presentation, you explain how dark colors absorb more light and heat. Your classmates are fascinated, and your teacher gives you a high-five for your clear explanation.

13. Think About How Science Changes the World
In fifth grade, you'll learn about scientific discoveries that changed history. Think about how science solves problems and improves lives.

Real-Life Scenario:
You read about how scientists created vaccines to fight diseases. It inspires you to think, "What problems could I solve with science in the future?" Maybe you'll be the next great inventor!

Final Thought
Fifth grade science is your chance to think like a scientist, explore exciting topics, and discover how the world works. By staying curious, working hard, and embracing challenges, you'll not only succeed in class but also learn skills that will last a lifetime. So put on your thinking cap, grab your lab notebook, and get ready for an awesome year of science. You've got this, future scientist!

Chapter 11 How to Succeed in Science in Fifth Grade

```
S Y M S T R N W Q R R M R X M Y X C D S F A O
D Q D H U X R A E G C X F W G B J Y Q Q I S M
Z O W E A H G V A W A M I R Q S X R Z R N J U
D S A P P S O N N J N D N S F Q Z U O R P H S
W D C L F C T D A A W C W U N U E V E G N X P
C D D I S F W U L L G E Y O D X H T X P I G G
D K O I E Y H M Y N T N E I Y E T U A M L C M
L J D C A N W C Z L U S V R U A N B V S T Q A
Y O A Y P G C W E K K G Y U P H Q D S I D K K
S T N E M I R E P X E D D C H Y P M T Q N I J
C E L A C I T I R C D L Z K S G K W K X X I S
K T Z J X N T I M L Y H X T I W R N B M U F A
W C T I R Q P E G K Q V S N O I T C E N N O C
Q A O L N H G I V L X O C N T X A P P Q G G B
V T T L D A Y A P D O C F M V V I S Y Q U M H
B A X H L W G G F N P A E E U E P T U O T A T
Q D H Y I A H R J R F B T T X M U R T I O Z F
S J N O K N B G O F R U A L R C T M J U B T U
Z G F J E Z K O L P X L Y X X Y P U R U S I Y
K T B R P C C I R K W A T Z B B H X Q W E X R
D E W T Y I S I N A Y R K T U G A C E O R S E
I M V V I Y H V J G T Y N M P N G G B J V M G
O D Z C J U A X Q Z S E V O P H H J F Q E N U
```

analyze	curious	organize
apps	data	patterns
collaborate	discover	science
connections	experiments	thinking
critical	observe	vocabulary

Chapter 12
How to Succeed in Writing in Fifth Grade

Hey, fifth-grade author! Writing in fifth grade is about more than just putting words on paper. You'll tackle creative stories, persuasive essays, research reports, and even poetry. Writing in fifth grade means developing your own voice, learning to organize your ideas, and making your words stand out. It might seem challenging at first, but with a little practice (and the tips in this chapter), you'll be ready to impress your teacher, your classmates, and even yourself. Ready to turn your ideas into amazing writing? Let's get started!

1. Start With a Strong Plan
Before you start writing, spend a few minutes planning. A strong plan can save you time and frustration later. Use a brainstorming chart, outline, or graphic organizer to jot down your ideas.

Real-Life Scenario:
You're assigned an essay about your favorite season. Instead of jumping straight into writing, you brainstorm reasons you love summer: swimming, ice cream, and no school! Then you organize them into an outline. When you start writing, your ideas flow easily because you already know what to say.

2. Create Catchy Beginnings
Your introduction is like the first bite of a delicious meal, it makes your reader want more. Start with a question, an interesting fact, or an exciting moment to grab attention.

Real-Life Scenario:
Instead of starting your story with, "I went to the amusement park," try: "The roller coaster loomed ahead, its steel tracks twisting into the sky like a giant metal snake. Was I brave enough to ride it?" Now your reader is hooked and wants to find out what happens next.

3. Add Details That Bring Your Writing to Life
Good writing paints a picture in the reader's mind. Use specific details, sensory words, and examples to make your writing vivid.

Real-Life Scenario:
You're writing about a trip to the beach. Instead of saying, "The water was cold," write, "The icy waves splashed against my toes, sending a shiver up my spine." Your classmates will feel like they're right there with you.

4. Organize Your Ideas Clearly
In fifth grade, your writing needs to have a clear structure. Use paragraphs to separate your ideas and transition words like first, next, then, and finally to guide your reader.

Real-Life Scenario:
You're writing a persuasive essay about why your school should have longer recess. In the first paragraph, you explain how recess helps kids focus. In the next, you talk about exercise. Finally, you wrap it up by saying longer recess would make everyone happier. Your essay is easy to follow, and your points are strong.

5. Use Dialogue to Make Characters Come Alive
When writing stories, use dialogue to show how characters think, feel, and interact. Remember to use quotation marks and make the conversation sound realistic.

Real-Life Scenario:
In your story, instead of writing, "Lila was scared," you write:
"'Do we really have to go in there?' Lila whispered, her voice trembling. 'It's so dark!'"
Your reader can feel her fear without you even saying it directly.

6. Mix Up Your Sentences

Good writing isn't just about what you say, it's about how you say it. Use short, punchy sentences for action and longer ones for description. Varying your sentence length keeps your writing interesting.

Real-Life Scenario:
Your teacher gives you this sentence to revise: "The dog ran across the yard." You rewrite it as: "The big, fluffy dog dashed across the wide, green yard, his tail wagging like a flag in the wind." Now your sentence has personality!

7. Edit Like a Pro

Even professional writers don't get it perfect the first time. Editing helps you spot mistakes, improve sentences, and make your writing shine. Use a checklist to make sure you've covered everything.

Real-Life Scenario:
You finish a story about a camping trip but realize you wrote "their" instead of "there" in two places. After fixing it and adding more details about the campfire, your story goes from good to great.

8. Back Up Your Opinions with Evidence

When writing persuasive essays, it's important to support your opinion with facts, examples, and reasons. This makes your argument stronger.

Real-Life Scenario:
You're writing about why kids should have less homework. Instead of just saying, "It's boring," you write, "Studies show that too much homework can cause stress and take away time for family and hobbies." Now your essay is more convincing.

9. Use Technology to Boost Your Writing

In fifth grade, you might use a computer or tablet to type your essays. Use spell check and online tools to polish your work, but don't rely on them too much—always review your writing yourself.

Real-Life Scenario:

You type a research report on volcanoes and use an online thesaurus to find a stronger word than "big." You replace it with "massive," making your report sound more professional.

10. Share Your Writing

Writing is meant to be shared! Whether it's reading your story to the class, publishing a poem in the school newsletter, or showing your essay to your family, sharing your work helps you feel proud of what you've created.

Real-Life Scenario:

You write a poem about friendship and read it aloud during a school assembly. The applause makes you feel like a real poet, and you can't wait to write another.

11. Learn From Feedback

When your teacher or classmates give you feedback, see it as a chance to grow. Pay attention to what they liked and what they think you could improve.

Real-Life Scenario:

Your teacher says your essay has great ideas but needs stronger transitions. You add phrases like, for example, and on the other hand, your next draft flows much better.

12. Practice, Practice!
The more you write, the better you'll get. Practice by keeping a journal, writing stories for fun, or even creating a comic strip. Every bit of practice makes a difference.

Real-Life Scenario:
You decide to write a short story every week in your notebook. By the end of the semester, you notice your characters are more interesting, and your plots have better twists. Practice really pays off!

Final Thought
Writing in fifth grade is your chance to share your ideas, explore your creativity, and develop skills that will last a lifetime. By planning carefully, using details, and embracing feedback, you'll become a confident writer who can tackle any assignment. So, grab a pencil (or a keyboard), unleash your imagination, and get ready to create something amazing. You've got this, fifth-grade author!

Chapter 12 How to Succeed in Writing in Fifth Grade

```
Q G A Q K R B D W L E G K I Z E B N D M V C S
G N T O M K K D Q E N N P T U A M I E W A E U
O S D E H S N K K G I A P F P X N Z E D H B T
S H O E G F S F R B K I L Y T O K Z X M P U C
Z J P Y Y A B N S H A R E P A Y I X J E B F Q
O C K C A B D E E F D O V S R N H A G H D F B
W P J O R W Y L Y S Z N Q Y A R Q C A O T I E
J A M E Z G V N J F Y U S G D L O Y T Z M I T
Q U Y G D J W C A G A E R X D X Y L I A D L H
Q D B L G U Y V H G N O Q X Y H D Z Y E C V B
U N S E R Y F A V T D S G N W O Y G A M X P P
I N P Z H A H K E R S K G Q K D P S U C S C W
Q D Q B K E E N E E E V F M F V Q Q S G L B D
X G W L R F C L Z N F T U R Z I F L P N I R L
K N L B O E F O C W S X U G C C Y P Z I A A T
O Y L G S Y I T I T L E Y P F W R I F T T C B
O X K C H J I C Y B V A A Z M A B N G I E B C
V G B S C G A I M I G D H E C O L N M R D U C
K L Q T A A P Y D X K Y K T X B C L J W X Y N
W Y T T H X D E P M R M I Q V P D O I E B F T
E K Z O S E N J T U Z C D Y A L H N H W A Y B
L E D H E C Z X G E E U X E U G O L A I D X B
F F T T E W F N G Q O R Q B D Z G W U D M E N
```

catchy	edit	plan
clearly	evidence	practice
computer	feedback	sentences
details	ideas	share
dialogue	organize	writing

Chapter 13
How to Master Homework in Fifth Grade

Hey there, fifth-grade homework champ! Homework in fifth grade can feel like a bigger deal than it did last year. It's longer, harder, and sometimes it feels like your teachers are giving you way too much. But guess what? You're older, smarter, and ready to tackle it like a pro. With a few strategies and the right attitude, you can handle anything that ends up in your backpack. This chapter is packed with tips, tricks, and real-life fifth-grade scenarios to help you master your homework and still have time for fun. Let's dive in!

1. Create a Homework Routine That Works for You
In fifth grade, sticking to a routine makes homework feel less overwhelming. Choose a time and place that works best for you and make it a habit.

Real-Life Scenario:
You decide to start your homework every day at 4:00 PM, right after you have a snack. You work at the kitchen table because it's quiet and your parents are nearby if you need help. After a week of doing this, it becomes part of your day, and you feel less stressed.

2. Write It Down Before You Forget
Your homework assignments might come from different teachers or cover multiple subjects, so it's easy to forget something. Keep a planner or notebook to write everything down.

Real-Life Scenario:
Your math teacher assigns a worksheet, and your science teacher tells you to bring in materials for an experiment. You write both in your planner before you leave class. Later, when you open your planner, you remember everything—and avoid that panicked "Oh no!" moment.

3. Break It Into Smaller Pieces
Some fifth-grade assignments take more time, especially big projects. Instead of trying to do everything at once, break your work into smaller steps.

Real-Life Scenario:
You're assigned a book report that's due in two weeks. Instead of waiting until the last minute, you plan it out:

- **Day 1:** Read the first few chapters.
- **Day 3:** Write notes about the main characters.
- **Day 5:** Start your rough draft.

By spreading out the work, the project feels manageable.

4. Eliminate Distractions
Distractions are your biggest enemy when it comes to homework. Put away your phone, turn off the TV, and find a quiet place to focus.

Real-Life Scenario:
You're working on a social studies assignment, but your little sibling keeps asking questions. You decide to move to your room, close the door, and finish your work in half the time because you're focused.

5. Start With the Hardest Task
When you have a long list of assignments, start with the hardest or most time-consuming one first. Your brain is freshest at the beginning, so tackle the tough stuff while you're still sharp.

Real-Life Scenario:
You have math problems, a spelling worksheet, and a short essay to write. You decide to do the math first because it's the hardest. Once it's done, the other tasks feel easier, and you finish faster.

6. Use a Homework Buddy

Sometimes, working with a friend can make homework more fun and less stressful. Choose a buddy who takes their work seriously and helps you stay on track.

Real-Life Scenario:

You and your friend decide to quiz each other on science vocabulary over video chat. They help you remember tricky terms like photosynthesis and ecosystem. By the end, you both feel ready for the test.

7. Don't Be Afraid to Ask for Help

If you're stuck, don't waste an hour staring at your paper. Ask for help from a teacher, parent, or even a classmate. Asking questions shows you care about doing it right.

Real-Life Scenario:

You can't figure out a tricky fraction problem. Instead of guessing, you ask your dad to explain it. He shows you a step-by-step way to solve it, and suddenly fractions aren't so scary.

8. Check Your Work Before You Finish

In fifth grade, your teachers expect fewer careless mistakes. Before you say "done," check your answers, spelling, and grammar to make sure everything is correct.

Real-Life Scenario:

You finish your geography worksheet but notice you labeled a state capital wrong. After fixing it, you feel proud handing in a perfect assignment.

9. Make Homework Fun (Yes, It's Possible!)
Turn boring assignments into a game. Use colored pens to highlight important points, set a timer to beat your record, or reward yourself when you finish.

Real-Life Scenario:
You decide to use different-colored highlighters for each part of your science notes—pink for vocabulary, blue for facts, and yellow for questions. Suddenly, your notes look cool and help you remember the information.

10. Stay Organized
Keep your homework in a folder or binder so it doesn't get lost in your backpack. An organized system helps you feel less stressed and more in control.

Real-Life Scenario:
Your classmate can't find their math homework because it's crumpled at the bottom of their bag. You smile, knowing your math worksheet is neatly tucked into your "Math" folder, ready to hand in.

11. Take Breaks When You Need To
If you have a lot of homework, take short breaks to rest your brain. A 5-minute stretch or snack can help you refocus.

Real-Life Scenario:
You're halfway through your spelling sentences and start feeling tired. You take a quick break to grab a drink of water and stretch. When you sit back down, you finish the rest in no time.

12. Celebrate Your Hard Work

When you finish all your homework, give yourself a little reward. Whether it's playing outside, watching your favorite show, or enjoying a snack, celebrating keeps you motivated.

Real-Life Scenario:
You complete all your assignments before dinner and have 30 extra minutes to play video games. You feel proud and realize that working hard pays off.

13. Learn From Mistakes

Not every homework assignment will be perfect, and that's okay. If you make a mistake, learn from it and try to do better next time.

Real-Life Scenario:
You lose points on your essay because you forgot to proofread. Next time, you double-check for grammar mistakes and earn an "A." Learning from the mistake helps you improve.

Final Thought

Fifth-grade homework might feel like a challenge, but with a little planning, focus, and effort, you can handle anything your teacher throws at you. By staying organized, asking for help when needed, and celebrating your wins, you'll master your assignments and still have time for fun. So grab your planner, sharpen your pencil, and show homework who's boss. You've got this, fifth-grade superstar!

Chapter 13 How to Master Homework in Fifth Grade

```
M M I S T A K E S J Q N N B U D D Y H G R P Z
P S F M E F G T O D J P O R T X V M Y G E A Z
X E K A O T Z Q S V F N E E I Z V H G T Z Z O
P C J L V H Q Q O U Z L H A U G B I D O J J S
V E F L H Q Y U K F O C C K H U T G L T I E I
H I Z E E O S Z S H J J Y S V S O H N L E R I
G P Y R S S M E A U L Z I B R X N L W B A O W
D O V Z U F B E E H P F V I V E H I P J U R Z
R N A R A O M Y W A N M F B J A H G M I M G J
U B V L O A H B F O R B S K B L C H E C K A K
A X K K Z U A O G C R O U I P E B T V X W N F
C T W J T D T G O X M K O H L U R R M K O I N
B L K F J S N I V T W L B T A P Q K F F D Z J
F T P V B M P G N B N T B P N E H N I B G E J
R O D Q G I C B A E N R V Q N K T T Q L R D L
Q V B D S A A C Q L E U X H E R A G H Q A Y U
V P C D L P P R N O L T E A R I A C D E K E V
Z L B F X O X B I E A Y E R Q T D L R Z L W K
O D N Q Z E U C P V N U C D G O T R Z M T P U
P V B R O T P M A D J A M E O H C O D T Y R Q
S R Y S H H M W X X M W P S E Z T Y V F K Y W
G G N W U T A O Y Q K K J T X J Q T O C K R E
J B F J F D H R G B R T G O D Z T O N H F P N
```

ask	hardest	organized
breaks	help	pieces
buddy	highlight	planner
check	homework	routine
first	mistakes	smaller

Chapter 14
How to Study for Exams in Fifth Grade

Hey there, fifth-grade superstar! Exams might sound a little scary, but they're just a way for you to show off what you've learned. With the right tools and strategies, you can go into any test feeling confident and ready to succeed. In fifth grade, studying for exams is a little different—it's not just about remembering facts; it's about understanding big ideas and connecting them. This chapter is packed with tips, tricks, and real-life fifth-grade scenarios to help you rock your next exam. Let's get started!

1. Know What to Study
Before you even start studying, make sure you know exactly what will be on the exam. Ask your teacher for a study guide or review what you've covered in class to focus on the most important topics.

Real-Life Scenario:
Your teacher says the science test will cover ecosystems, food chains, and photosynthesis. You check your notes and highlight these sections to study. When you take the test, you feel confident because you focused on the right material.

2. Create a Study Schedule
In fifth grade, exams might cover more material than before, so cramming the night before won't cut it. Spread your studying over several days to give your brain time to absorb the information.

Real-Life Scenario:
Your social studies test is next week, so you plan to study a little each day. On Monday, you review maps. On Tuesday, you go over explorers. By Thursday, you feel ready and relaxed instead of rushed and panicked.

3. Start With What You Don't Know
It's tempting to review the stuff you already know, but studying what you find tricky will help you the most. Focus on your weak spots first.

Real-Life Scenario:
You're great at multiplication but struggle with fractions. Instead of spending hours on multiplication, you practice adding and subtracting fractions until it starts to make sense. On test day, you feel ready for anything.

4. Use Flashcards
Flashcards are a great way to memorize facts, vocabulary, or formulas.
- Supplies Needed: Index cards (any size of your choice)
- Write a question or term on one side of an index card and the answer on the flip side.
- After creating the flashcard, read the question and then the answer.
- Read both sides of the card without trying to memorize the answer.
- Repeat the above step over and over
- Do this repeatedly each day. Soon you'll realize that you know the information without really trying to memorize it.
- Test yourself or ask a friend or family member to quiz you.
- **This works!**

Real-Life Scenario:
You use flashcards to study history dates, like "What year was the Declaration of Independence signed?" When your dad quizzes you, you say, "1776!" and feel proud of how much you remember.

5. Try Study Games
Who says studying has to be boring? Turn it into a game! Make up trivia questions, play memory match, or challenge a friend to a quiz-off.

Real-Life Scenario:
You and a classmate create a science trivia game using index cards. Each correct answer earns a point. By the end, you've had fun and reviewed everything for your test.

6. Use Practice Tests
Practice tests are a great way to get ready for the real thing. If your teacher doesn't give you one, make your own by turning key points into questions.

Real-Life Scenario:
You write down questions from your math textbook, like "What's 12 × 8?" and "How do you convert 3/4 to a decimal?" When you finish answering, you check your work and feel ready for the real test.

7. Use Visuals
Drawings, charts, and diagrams can help you understand tough topics. If you're a visual learner, turn your notes into something colorful and fun to look at.

Real-Life Scenario:
You're studying the water cycle. Instead of just reading your notes, you draw a diagram showing evaporation, condensation, and precipitation. When you see the question on the test, you picture your drawing and answer confidently.

8. Teach Someone Else
If you can explain a concept to someone else, it means you really understand it. Teach a sibling, friend, or even your pet!

Real-Life Scenario:
You explain the food chain to your little brother, starting with producers and ending with predators. He asks, "So, are humans predators?" and you realize you've got the whole concept down.

9. Take Study Breaks
Your brain needs time to recharge, especially when you're studying for a big exam. Study for 25-30 minutes, then take a 5-10 minute break to stretch, grab a snack, or relax.

Real-Life Scenario:
You're reviewing spelling words and feel that your focus is slipping. You take a short break to play with your dog, then return to your desk refreshed and ready to finish strong.

10. Make Connections
In fifth grade, exams often test how well you can connect ideas. Don't just memorize facts—think about how they fit together and why they're important.

Real-Life Scenario:
You're studying explorers and realize that many of them were looking for new trade routes. You connect this to the geography lessons about maps and realize why they risked their lives for their journeys. The big picture helps you remember the details.

11. Stay Calm and Confident

The night before the exam, review lightly, get a good night's sleep, and eat a healthy breakfast. Go into the test believing in yourself—you've worked hard, and you're ready.

Real-Life Scenario:
On the morning of your math test, you tell yourself, "I studied. I've got this." You feel calm and focused, and you tackle the test one question at a time.

12. Learn From Mistakes

Not every test will be perfect, and that's okay. When you get your results back, look at what you missed and learn from it so you're ready for next time.

Real-Life Scenario:
You miss a question about the phases of the moon because you mixed up waxing and waning. Your teacher explains it, and you draw a quick sketch in your notebook to remember it for the future.

Final Thought

Studying for exams in fifth grade is about more than just remembering facts—it's about understanding the big ideas, staying organized, and giving yourself enough time to prepare. With these tips, you'll feel confident and ready to show what you've learned. So, grab your notes, make a plan, and get to work—you've got this, fifth-grade superstar!

Chapter 14 How to Study for Exams in Fifth Grade

```
W N G Z Y A K O J Z O B Q X E P S K A E R B F
U F I D B F T G G N R C N T L J K A E W N G L
S A P A X L D A J L F N W G U T K X P T H F A
V I H F J T S J B N O Z K Z D M V G F D K C S
C O N F I D E N T E G T T S E T P X A O H J H
S A I F R K Q V Z J Q N X Y H J E X A M S V C
E T Y T A I H E V G G X T Q C I I L J I E F A
H S S N K M H J U U K X Y T S A P N O S S S R
H K D E N W G Y B S Y D P K J L O A V S K X D
X D V J T P P E C T K R H H U F D V S C M W S
J R N S D H M A C U R R U L T P O V T I D B G
Q A P C B G Y Z A D P Q W H U R T V C V W X C
I B U W Y N A M M Y B B H S P G O U D O R O C
G R X K J M C V N V B S B N W Q H N X J Z N C
J N I B Z Q B O V J N W W O F A X U Y D E W B
B E U X O L V G K C A L M I B U B M P U V M O
Z T C Y J A A Z Z R A M O T D O L C P U I W E
S O R I S Q H Q N J F I K C X S J P S G S L G
D B E B T L S D X N S S X E G A Z Q Y J U K A
O E F O Z C I Y I V T C Z N F P R Q N D A C Z
G D E X P L A I N Z O D H N J Z Y B L O L A W
U L J M M J Q R A Y P T O O C Q B H I C S R O
Z V T L R N Z W P K S A R C A K N Q L D E V E
```

breaks	explain	spots
calm	flashcards	study
confident	games	tests
connections	practice	visuals
exams	schedule	weak

WORD SEARCH SOLUTIONS

Chapter 1 How to Crush the First Day of Fifth Grade

```
E K B I N E M P Z A Q P Q V K V E I Z N W Q S
Y J F N Q Z L R G O N J W O M V L E K W A D K
L C N K G F S D D X W E P U I G U E B G I G Z
U I N D Q A F X X A S Z H T M R L Q M Z L B E
K D L E F B O I X Q Y V I D N I U D Y S E Z G
L C E W L J E V E F Y S Y O U R S E L F T F R
O V A U M O X C E E O Z I M Y O U T O F B J
S B D K N H R O Z P G T U W K D S Z V P F W W
B V E B U B I C M H A K Z O V X E A V A O V
J V R T B W E X K R J A M V M U O S E T W F U
C D S O G A L P A F L E X I B L E D E F H A
J C H V H S C P A E Q F V I S C H I P I W M V
P V I Y V E B K Z A V X P Y G T Y R X N D S
Z I P E B R P N Q L Q H G J R U K S I O S J J
O V G G P L L G I F B J L A D M T P B E V U X
Y T T Y Q H F Q T G E D E H D U S G W W P V
O K C D H L A E Y U U E Y H A Y P N B M R Z T
V A E C Q B N R M S Z O N Y S W E C W U K T R
N L N F X I R C G C R J R G T L N M O H T K Y
K T N U H M V G E S P V E K L N H T O S Y T
G W O S H I Z F Y U U O G A Y Q E F O J V O Y
R Y C E K O T I M A F L H T K S C H E D U L E
V E O Q W I S K W D B C F T X L C X O B L T G
```

Chapter 2 How to Pick the Right Friends in Fifth Grade

```
K V U L T U E N B H J J J F I N S J J G M H I
T A L O W C B X U H V S N U Q C F H Q J C Y B
H A N Y C J I E C Z N H W G F L A O G O E S P
V C K A U H V E O D V P A F W A V U Z Y B K V
B I M L V G J X M A T O C X W K X O E G S U K
U C A T J R J C P P R I D U X P Z O N F W C X
R Z K Y F E P O R I U C U I G X Y H D A O I W
O R L A M W L I O H S D K M R Q G E I D R P A
H C R D I O M N M S T B A M A R D X F W G C C
G R X V G I T C I D S F T R H G W Y H K Y Q C
E D S I K J S O S N T D O P H T I A Y Z X D X
Z S Z W G H E Y E E I M T U M F I L S A U B A
I E B X Y Y C F F I W I L U S P Q M M L Z S I
P K S L W O N Z A R G X R B I O H E H K C E A
J N D U N T E P V F I P F R Q N G Y Z C Z Q B
S Y N J D V R V R Y T H C K O A O W V I I B Y
K U E F P W E M C T J U O E R P P F W P N N S
E P I V C J F N W Y D J Y U P I T V V G L T F
F Y R X D L F E S U P P O R T E D J L P T B F
D J F U O F I U L Q N C D M N H L A U G H U U
F Q I X L F D V T S N K A J B J G K L A C A V
X K F Z S U N Y J E R Y X C M M H I O O R Z Q
A F I V P L U Y M A D N Y A V L K P R J C U S
```

Chapter 3 How to Handle Disagreements in the Fifth Grade Classroom

```
A C R J S O Y L H L T Z N V Z G U M Y S U J G
Z D D N Y O N G R J I K O G P K B I V K U C D
K Q K M O Z T E O L N S B E G L E H W L O N I
A G V H N N M U O Y Q I T Z X V K U Q Z G M Z
E D X C R J B K S N U Q U E N A Z P F N D A Z
R S X F A E C O P J O D S M N J C R G H R G I
B J H F E E B G H P R N B O N N L F B T E G D
I C Q T L R S T N E M E R G A S I D S S Q D
U F W Y Z I J Q A Z D P O G X V O R Q D P V W
Q M F E G Z P R U N N J S D I X Z K Q R E X G
M R E M F Q N W G N Z K Y B Z Y S B M L C R N
E W J K K X A E X A L W N H E T M O B V T F W
K T Q T J T Z I X R I A F V B M W J S G D T H
A P W M O F D C J M Q E Y M S O L U T I O N I
T E N F N R N C C R J N W X H U H S N G W O R
S F G V Q G O R E E H Y A U X H T R E U M W A
I Y I C E G C M Q S K R I M H K S R M U D E W
M F Q T T P E R S P E C T I V E V X E M C F F
C X A I U I H H F W H I X B Y M Y Y T Z Q T P
T A T Z D V N M N W E H D Q Z R Z Y A C A L M
G E K J R N B M I F N D B B K N U Y T J E Z Q
L M P H U M O R C S K E U X Y J D S S H T Q Y
W G V R S G U K R Q H W U Z Z O J E I M V A L
```

Chapter 4 Handling Disagreements on the Playground in Fifth Grade

```
R A H M W N T V O R N R K V D F O E B H Z W A
Y Z W R P B R H F Z Z O M M I O V D S W F X Q
W T O S X G N Z L Z G R I K H I P T C L K X L
C F B S H J I A Q I H F F N T W A K M Z L V E
O E T O T W M F U H T X K A Y D L S S F I T
M P L I Z R I T I O R D E E C P I O F Q S U Y
P E V O L R Y V A Z Y R Y O N Y O L R L N X U
R A E G R T T G E R C P O K E W P P N Q F G
O C H S J N P Y L C R L L P T E U Y J Q R O S
M E Q E J E H T Y F P B U C X E P T Y Y Z T K
I M P H K N A I O M L Z H O W X W F R C R Z T
S A L P G O H R Z D A Z Z A B C C R M A H X F
E K B D Z Y L U N A Y E M M Q K N T T Y L Z B
G E R N T R B T G G G B O W Y T P E T C J U Z
P R C E X E P A Y U R O G F Q H G I W P B D C
D Y I P C V I M Z V O P H Z T I O K I B S C T
X A V M Q E A I T R U E X Q E U Y G W L Q X N
Q W Z I J K S E K U N B Z S H I Q E C X G Y R
W A M I M W C S V G D A J W U K J V R X E L O
V K U W O N G A V M W U N H V N U U C D C G
V L E O D B V Q Q I F V P W K H F J L W N V Y
M A F Q E E J Z X L V W B J R E Z K E F Y D N
F W B R L F Z I A T Z K S A E N E N S C I T U
```

Chapter 5 How to Ask the Right Questions in Fifth Grade

```
E C U F E A X O J X H M V I H J K H D W R H D
N J G T G I Y B Z K U M E E B T A P F B I J W
N S Q P O I J B H O L V P E K O R Z R Q L H X
G H R I E D K T D S O W F P L E E S L V F K Z
R C U D I M Q J O N P I A M H C Y N Y G A Y R
T L G H S I N T O O E K S G Q K S O L G X H H
P G G F Q S X Q T I N K M T J B S I Z C S C T
A C C F M T G L N T E T F D H P V T R H F B W
B E O D S A E S E S N B Q H E D U C L A K V W
D R B X B K X I D E D O T C P Y A E T L S U K
T W I B E E H D I U E I I O K Z D N L L P O T
H O W C N S J A F O D F T K E C N J E X H C
D U F H A U T N T I M Z F A C O O Z N G I I
Y A G L O V N S O C Z Y B A M M U C M G X Q U
M S G X H L W T C A G S H V R N R R I C Y I
Z O N N D R E C E X I O M T D W C O Z N Q Y D
O J I H R N A L X K T R C E L R O H F G S B X
B X N K R T Y A V M F E R Q W I B K H N I S T
Z V E E J J X S B H K S W C H T Z R A L I W C
P F T F J D G S B V T T F O A E C M Z U O P E
K L S I X R J M K A B M H B N W Y Y M A R B Y
G U I G A Q M A N P X M J V F O L L O W U P W
Q R L V D B G D S A W T E C H N O L O G Y W M
```

124

Chapter 6 How to Rock Small Group Work in Fifth Grade

```
G G U I B L T D S W S W C D E X L P F P N D G
Y G N A L P S I D H R O T E Z Y Q D Z X N Q K
R R Q J I A M G I Y Y R D A Y B E C T V Q I E
T O Z E E F A V X M T I R I A Z V I W E O L M
T U U D H B C V C D V J T I M X I W U T B K H
T P I Z C Z N M Y I R X E M B A E E A N E R T
N S C R V R T O D U I B P D O Q A P B O U R N
F I X P T T C N S E C N E R E F F I D P Q I U
A Z B Q P D E Y O B S F H F F O C U S E D S D
I X F R L F P R J Z V J M P Y J Y E Q N W U K
R K K E Q T S N S Q X O V N J A T X V Z B Z M
L Z U S M N E Q D A S T R E N G T H S E H U F
Y C T P O E R P E D B F L G L N X V Y S P F C
P R F O O M L S D T B C K J F E N I R I T I U
S F N N R E Q D Q V Z A W E E A X V S P F R K
D S V S S G F B C Y W L Z G D W K F F S S Z H
I Y A I S A R A K D W M L X V J R H N P Q H B
X P D B A R X X I K V L L S V D U Z E O P R C
U M D I L U S V O G N Y B F J F M A F M A C H
R Q T L C O I E H I D J M P H T K M V K C R C
M W A I X C E F V A F I F P M U T E J J Q Z R
F E O T P N W N V M E S V F P O G D F B I P M
P D S Y E E W S M A L L A S S N X N Y W R T D
```

125

Chapter 7 How to Succeed in Studying History in Fifth Grade

```
Y T Y Z P L J W W I J W F W O F Y C Z O D J C
J U I Z L P C M P Q A Z Z I C W P R S I H F R
Q G S T G V G P L T A C T J A Z C V O M K C E
Q Z T N N B I H N R I P K L L G D C I T U C S
D O C U M E N T A R I E S E F T G Y E R S N S
M W A F Q O D B F T I G Q W W U J A R O E I H
A Q F R I O B L P Z T L A X S C W E L G C V H
J S X C Y Y S U B K J Z Q I I J N W D P R M B
V B Q H H L S R T M Y L I V W T Y S I J U O Z
R L L M X U U H W V Q A M M V H F G P I O T H
Y T K E T G T V S P O U C U B I D X P J S I X
L J O I L Q S A D M K E K V E D O D U Q M G
R C S I U R A U A V G M H S R P E E J F A E O
K I Y G N L W W C V K A L G T P F V O L P L H
V B H H B H L U C L N A P J H I N I E S M I Q
U K P T W A Z S V E J G Y N E H O N U N D N S
H D I S C U S S I O N S I C Z U A N M G T E L
U W A C E C I T C A R P O H T E U F S P O S T
C B A J H I N H C U I P W A T D W N Z V X N B
A P R X T G U G C J L J M G G T C T O C S Z Q
P R I M A R Y V T H I N Y S O C U K R O N Y O
C S I L O O B V K X V O R N D T A C Y A H D C
L A N O S R E P Z K A Y V Y R O T S H X R W H
```

Chapter 8 How to Master Fifth Grade Math

```
R S X F A T P J D C S U N B O O F N K K U N X
C O S C I N B F V O U E Z X Q Y I P M I W V R
R K M P V S X D D U M J R Q I H Q E P C K E J
D N W I P L Q T Q M E B V U F A A C H H A K D
H T N E Q T Y G W X G I Y R O D B A X L D I H
F J T H J R J Q H L S C A S Y M L H L V G F E
W S M V I V S N U U A C E G Z L D I U F Q D R
E V S I C T H J A R T Y D W E U F W C J B E B
S M B D S B W L L I M P W N R E R G I U R Q L
Q H I Y I T Z V O S R W G Q F X W V U N T J O
C U R U P I A N N Q I E D T I T V J S S R O X
W A E N V V S K I N A Y R T E M O E G D Q R T
O E C S H T Y F E L D E C I M A L S V C C V O
L B B G T L Y I Q S G T E C S Y W I J K E G O
O W I S W I E K F N P L U U Y B H G C G N M L
C C C N I P O S E P S P O A P E R E L L A M S
I D X H E T J N O B H U K W T V I K M R R R D
C M H G B Y E S P K T K M D G M R K R I W L
N K Q X L J T S T W C D C R W T Q A M D D Z T
L T H N T Q Y A D I P P E D B Q W H T C W F Y
C S W P Z O N K A E J T H G F J P L Q H A S V
G Y E T L D Z T O U P W C D N A T S R E D N U
F H F L Z X V Z Y J Y B L O L H Z N B Q D Y E
```

Chapter 9 How to Succeed in Reading in Fifth Grade

```
W G P Z O S F B A O Q Y W J G R M H B T R Z C
Q B O X R L N R I V U I P C K I H H D W I W I
P K P Y J A E A N O R E U Q H R V A M K H H Y
L V J T R O D U X C B O R W Z C L Q C Q U H Y
E D N S B G A C A P F U P L O Z P G G A G O B
E N D G E P E G V D N H O T N O T E S I E Q Q
C J N D R M R W Y X J Q S C P A C Q C O N W N
C Y B V Z P E E A H X A E U W Y S H M T R L B
I S E F C L R H D U F D G A S I J B I I E Y Z
Z R Z A S F D U T I O M Y Q S Y J Q O R S Y I
A Q I U F S D V B R C I X E J L E G J P H H V
C U L D T Y Y Q T Z W T J F L X T A L I E P O
L E A I S L D Q J Y E Y I N P B O W D M C S H
M S U O B H X D G A H X I O M A N C L E I M N
Q T S B O O K W O R M D P J N Q M K A V K E V
X I I O I A T K E B K H Y L B S Q O I Q A J V
H O V O R K E A S N D U Z N O P L H O R V R L
R N V K O X D D S J V X M R Z R T X D E D B A
X S N S V I M T U I C S T P H K E P Z E N E J
K N P U N J T C E A B C M B T H U Q B U U L Y
I I D G Y R A L U B A C O V Z K C X N K R G N
F R L B Q N C W K S H L D S J D C I U V V P O
E S S U C S I D Z P L C I D E T L G Z S W E I
```

Chapter 10 How to Succeed in Fifth Grade P.E.

```
C R V L Y G K C T Q Y T Q E R L O Z H Y I G X
A L I R C S H R P F L A R M W G D L U D R V V
U X Z R Y Y S C O V M O E O E T Y B F B P J D
Y L F O D M A U X W V H X F F C W W H M L P M
U B L R M F S I E F M E Z T R M I H W I O V M
R Z A O X X F Z O O R A Y Y Y F O G L B W G Z
O T A X V G Q H O K I L E W R H E C L E M H S
E J O A D E G O H Z D T J T I L T P E H A L X
Y D B N T A H C I V B H J S P K P T O V L I B
Y Z F E R R I B W H V Y W B D F C M L I S U Y
I E U K L O W P E L O H X Q E B F I K P F Z X
F X Q D P A V T S P O R T S M A N S H I P U C
V W X H A U V B O V E S U T S D O O F V B L L
R N Z V C A E I B F G E T A R B E L E C I V J
L D W W T E W C K M F W Z V F F I T N E S S B
E W X G I H G C J K E F T R J H U O N Y C D A
W G G Y V D H B R M S H J A R W N S J R U N D
W V D Z E L O X Q Q A M Q N J S P L V X J Z J
C H S R C P H Y S I C A L E D U C A T I O N K
B E X S U L B T S D B C E M G F Q O R F P L T
F O L E F L K X N W B L V G A N O G X F B K G
I E O X S Z E Y A I C F F N F D B B I F S G H
Y Y H Q Q W W S W J Y L R I A F F C R P J C E
```

Chapter 11 How to Succeed in Science in Fifth Grade

```
S Y M S T R N W O R R M R X M Y X C D S F A O
D Q D H U X R A E G C X F W G B J Y Q Q I S M
Z O W E A H G V A W A M I R Q S X R Z R N J U
D S A P P S O N N J N D N S F Q Z U O R P H S
W D C L E C T D A A W C W U N U E V E G N X P
C D D I S F W U L G E Y O D X H T X P I G G
D K O I E Y H M Y N T N E I Y E T U A M L C M
L J D C A N W C Z L U S V R U A B V S T Q A
Y O A Y P G C W E K K G Y U P H Q D S I D K K
S T N E M I R E P X E D D C H Y P M T Q N I J
C E L A C I T I R C D L Z K S G K W K X X I S
K T Z J X N T I M L Y H X T I W R N B M U F A
W C I R Q P E G K Q V S N O I T C E N N O C
Q A O L N H G I V L X O C N T X A P P Q G G B
V T T L D A Y A P D O C F M V V I S Y Q U M H
B A X H L W G F N P A E E U E P T U O T A T
Q D H Y I U R J R F B T T X M U R T I O Z F
S J N O K N B G O F R U A L R C T M J U B T U
Z G F J E Z R O L P X L Y X X Y P U R U S I Y
K T B R P C C I R K W A T Z B B H X Q W E X R
D E W T Y I S I N A Y R K T U G A C E O R S E
I M V V I Y H V J G T V N M P N G G B J V M G
O D Z C J U A X Q Z S E V O P H H J F Q E N U
```

Chapter 12 How to Succeed in Writing in Fifth Grade

```
Q G A Q K R B D W L E G K I Z E B N D M V C S
G N T O M K K D Q E N N P T U A M I E W A E U
O S D E H S N K K G I A P F P X N Z E D H B T
S H O E G F S F R B K I L Y T O K Z X M P U C
Z J P Y Y A B N S H A R E P A Y I X J E B F Q
O C K C A B D E E F D O V S R N H A G H D F B
W P J O R W Y L Y S Z N Q Y A R Q C A O T I E
J A M E Z G V N J F Y U S G D L O Y T Z M I T
Q U Y G D J W C A G A E R X D X Y L I A D L H
Q D B L G U Y V H G N O Q X Y H D Z Y E C V B
U N S E R Y F A V T D S G N W O Y G A M X P P
I N P Z H A H K E R S K G Q K D P S U C S C W
Q D Q B K E E N E E V F M F V Q Q S G L B D
X G W L R E C L Z N F T U R Z I F L P N I R L
K N L B O E F O C W S X U G C C Y P Z I A A T
O Y L G S Y I T I T L E Y P F W R I F T T C B
O X K C H J I C Y B V A A Z M A B N G I E B C
V G B S C G A I M I G D H E C O L N M R D U C
K L Q T A A P Y D X K Y K T X B C L J W X Y N
W Y T T H X D E P M R M I Q V P D O I E B F T
E K Z O S E N J T U Z C D Y A L H N H W A Y B
L E D H E C Z X G E E U X E U G O L A I D X B
F F T T E W F N G Q O R Q B D Z G W U D M E N
```

Chapter 13 How to Master Homework in Fifth Grade

```
M M I S T A K E S J Q N N B U D D Y H G R P Z
P S F M E F G T O D J P O R T X V M Y G E A Z
X E K A O T Z Q S V F N E E I Z V H G T Z Z O
P C J L V H Q Q O U Z L H A U G B I D O J J S
V E F L H O Y U K F O C C K H U T G L T I E I
H I Z E E O S Z S H J J Y S V S O H N L E R I
G P Y R S S M E A U L Z I B R X N L W B A O W
D O V Z U F B E H P F V I E H I P J U R Z
R N A R A O M Y W N M F B J A H G M I M G J
U B V L O A H B F O R B S K B L C H E C K A K
A X K K Z U A O G C R O U I P E B T V X W N F
C T W J T D T G O X M K O H L U R R M K O I N
B L K F J S N I T W L B T A P Q K F F D Z J
F T P V B M P G N B N T B P N E H N I B G E J
R O D Q G I C B A E N R V Q N K T T Q L R D L
Q V B D S A A C Q L E U X H E R A G H O A Y U
V P C D L P P R N O L T E A R I A C D E K E V
Z L B F X O X B I E A Y E R Q T D L R Z L W K
O D N Q Z E U C P V N U C D G O T R Z M T P U
P V B R O T P M A D J A M E O H C O D T Y R Q
S R Y S H H M W X X M W P S E Z T Y V F K Y W
G G N W U T A O Y Q K K J T X J Q T O C K R E
J B F J F D H R G B R T G O D Z T O N H F P N
```

Chapter 14 How to Study for Exams in Fifth Grade

```
W N G Z Y A K O J Z O B Q X E P S K A E R B F
U F I D B F T G G N R C N T L J K A E W N G L
S A P A X L D A J L F N W G U T K X P T H F A
V I H F J T S J B N O Z K Z D M V G F D K C S
C O N F I D E N T E G T T S E T P X A O H J H
S A I F R K Q V Z J Q N X Y H J E X A M S V C
E T Y T A I H E V G G X T Q C I I L J E F A
H S S N K M H J U U K X Y T S A P N O S S S R
H K D E N W G Y B S Y D P K J L O A V S K X D
X D V J T P P E C T K R H H U F D V S C M W S
J R N S D H M A C U R R U L T P O V T I D B G
Q A P C B G Y Z A D P Q W H U R T V C V W X C
I B U W Y N A M M V B B H S P G O U D O R O C
G R X K J M C V N V B S B N W Q H N X J Z N C
J N I B Z Q B O V J N W W O F A X U Y D E W B
B E U X O L V G K C A L M I B U B M P U V M O
Z T C Y J A A Z Z R A M O T D O L C P U I W E
S O R I S Q H Q N J F I K C X S J P S G S L G
D B E B T L S D X N S S X E G A Z Q Y J U K A
O E F O Z C I Y I V T C Z N F P R Q N D A C Z
G D E X P L A I N Z O D H N J Z Y B L O L A W
U L J M M J Q R A Y P T O O C Q B H I C S R O
Z V T L R N Z W P K S A R C A K N Q L D E V E
```

133

Other Books by Bobbie Anderson Jr.

- Third Grade Survival Guide
- Fourth Grade Survival Guide
- Sixth Grade Survival Guide

www.ingramcontent.com/pod-product-compliance
Lightning Source LLC
Chambersburg PA
CBHW051950290426
44110CB00015B/2188